How to Make Contacts and Win Friends

How to Make Contacts and Win Friends

Master the E-A-S-Y Method

Anyone can learn the H-C-Q-C Process

Carl Randolph
Inspirational Coach

©2014 Carl Randolph

All rights reserved. No part of this publication may be reproduced or distributed in any form or by any means, electronically or mechanically, including scanning, photocopying, recording, retrieval system, or otherwise without prior written permission from the author, except for the inclusion of brief quotes in a review.

Library of Congress Control Number: 2014902491

ISBN 978-1-4675-9935-1

Cover design by Aaron Randolph
/www.AaronRandolphsArt.Carbonmade.com/

Interior pictures by Aaron Randolph

Published by Carl Randolph
DeSoto, Texas

Quantity discounts are available on bulk purchases of this book for educational or gift purposes.

Request for permission to make copies of any part of this book can be made at Carl@CarlRandolph.net.

What are TOP leaders saying about *How to Make Contacts and Win Friends?*

"I have literally traveled all over the world teaching wealth and success principles and I found out that people are basically the same. They all want to succeed in life. Carl Randolph has been a personal friend for many, many years and his enthusiastic passion for helping others is definitely a cut above most people. *"How to Make Contacts and Win Friends"* has simple contacting techniques that everyone can learn. This book is right on time for anyone who needs to add more people to their business or company. Every business starts with a handshake. Allow Mr. Randolph to guide you through his step-by-step strategies to help you win big."

~Johnny D. Wimbrey
International Speaker and Best-Selling Author

"I have known Carl Randolph for over 30 years and was delighted to learn he has decided to write and release *"How to Make Contacts and Win Friends"*. This book is an excellent guide for anyone interested in making contacts and networking their way to success. You will find Carl's step by step, simple to execute techniques to be invaluable to you in your quest to grow individually or as a team through mastering the 'art of contacting'. I have read and believe that one of the best indicators of where one might expect to find him or herself five years from now will be largely determined by the books they read and the people they surround themselves with. This must read will save you time, energy and effort as Carl will help you overcome what could be considered by many one of the most difficult hurdles to overcome, and that is 'meeting people'. Reading and applying the strategies laid out by Carl will benefit you if you consider yourself a seasoned pro at 'contacting' people or an introvert like myself."

~Charles Prince
Owner-The Prince Group

"I recommend Carl Randolph and his instructions to anyone who wants to know how to make excellent contacts and turn them into friends. The practical information that he shares in his book will help you champion meeting people and turning them into long-term relationships."

~Tyrone Lister
International Speaker and Best-Selling Author

"An excellent read especially for those who dare to enter the world of network marketing. Carl Randolph gives a complete guide of the Do's and Don'ts of an industry that can set individuals and families financially free."

~Donald D. Bradley
Network Marketing Business Coach

"I have known Carl Randolph for a long time. Our families have known each other for over two decades. I have personally seen Mr. Randolph apply these principles in his daily life with true success. I encourage you to apply these teachings in your life personally and professionally. This book is a "must have" for your personal development library."

~Tracy D. Day
Financial Coach

"Carl definitely has the ability to connect with people. He is an expert in teaching what is essential to build a business, both offline and online. I highly recommend this book to anyone wanting to learn the key ingredient in business, which is being able to build relationships. Get it now and apply what you learn; you will definitely see a vast improvement in your life and your business."

~Karen Marrow
Internet Marketer

"I have read Carl Randolph's book "How to Make Contacts and Win Friends". As a motivational speaker, and one who has mentored many Sales Professionals in my 20 plus years in the Sales & Marketing arena, this is a must read and must have book for anyone in Sales of any kind. Carl's book masterfully provides the reader with critical steps to ensure their success in connecting and developing winning relationships. This book will become your roadmap, your personal "Blue Print" to this process. I have known Carl both personally and professionally for many years, and I have watched him successfully employ the many principles and techniques he highlights in this book."

~Henry R. Stinson, III
Business Owner

"As a former CFO, and a current consultant to the Fortune 500, I know the value of partnering with high-quality people, and Carl Randolph is one of the highest quality individuals I have ever had the pleasure of knowing. I have a great amount of respect for Mr. Randolph not only because he is very successful in his field, but also because of the man that he is. He knows how to help people take their life to a whole new level."

~Tim Jackson
Consultant to Fortune 1000 Companies

"For nearly 3 decades we've watched Carl's business success explode while implementing the very principles he teaches! "*How to Make Contacts and Win Friends*" is a must read for those who not only want to know **what** to do - but **how** to do...! This skills-to-paper book inspires one to believe that their next new friend - is truly a handshake away!"

~Bobby and Stacye Bowers
Owners, Your Travel Compass

"Carl Randolph is definitely the true definition of a contact King. I have had the pleasure in working with him for over 25 years and the results of his laboring have been phenomenal. He is a great industry leader, a loyal family man that is full of integrity. Not only in business, but consider him a great friend that loves helping others."

~Craig Sweet
Professional Networker

"I've had the pleasure of knowing and working with Carl in many different venues and he is ALWAYS super positive, on time and HUNGRY to make a difference in the lives of whoever is in the room!! His commitment to an extraordinarily high level of excellence in whatever he sets his mind to is simply inspiring!! You can't be an Eagle hanging around pigeons and Carl is an Eagle that is soaring high!!!"

~Ed Blunt
International Inspirational Speaker & Trainer

"If God ever created a perfect people person, it is Carl Randolph. By his mere entrance into a room he draws people to attention, excites them to enthusiastic response, and motivates them to action. In the years I have known Carl as a friend and fellow speaker; I have observed that what you see is what you get. Carl stands as a rock of integrity and what path he directs others to take he has already walked himself. You will enjoy Carl's sense of humor and his ability to tell stories with excitement and emotion. You will be more motivated to talk to people from any walk of life if you put Carl's principles into practice."

~Loretta Calhoun
Motivational Coach and Trainer

"Carl Randolph is an incredible teacher. He definitely knows how to change the surroundings around him when he enters your space. The people in his space will leave with a smile. He is making a difference, and I believe this book will be a big help to anyone looking to meet new people."

~Lee Lemons
International Recruiter Dallas, TX

"The Concept of the Book "*How to Make Contacts and Win Friends*" is an invaluable, simple, but awesome treasure of principles found in this book. Carl is more than qualified and capable to speak with his over 20 years' experience in the people business. This book should be in everyone's library. The book is well needed for anyone that wants to sharpen their skills in meeting new people. He leaves unique tools that enable individuals to understand why they should follow these steps to win. I believe that "*How to Make Contacts and Win Friends*" stands head and shoulders above the other books out there on the shelves. The principles are simple, but the results that you will achieve will be extraordinary."

~Pastor Everett Gilmore
Regional Director

Table of Contents

Foreword — 13

Acknowledgments — 15

Introduction — 17
    Get the Most Out of This Book

1. I Followed the System — 21
       Marketing Trends
       Change How You See Cold Marketing
       We All Have Filters
       People Are Looking
       It's All about Your Attitude

2. The Benefits of Networking — 29
       The Most Important Name
       Let Me Tell You a Little Story

3. How to Master the E-A-S-Y Method — 35
       How to Build Rapport
       Be in a Hurry
       Be Attentive to Gender and Other Dynamics
       Do's and Don'ts

4. The H-C-Q-C Process   46
    A Passionate Goal
    How the H-C-Q-C Process Works
    Exchange Contact Information

5. Make Contacts and Build Relationships   61
    Watch Your Personal Hygiene
    PI: The Pre-Impression
    First Impression
    Give Compliments
    Build Trust
    Connect with the Person
    Focusing on the Person
    You Will Experience Rejection
    Don't Be So Quick to Hand Out Your Business Card
    Organize Your Contacts

6. Top Places to Meet People and Make Friends   82
    Networking Tips
    Keep the Flow Moving
    Have a Few Exit Statements Ready
    Don't Be This Person

7. Personality Styles by Color   91
    Red – Blue – Yellow – Green
    How to Relate to the Different Colors

8. The Biggest Mistake People Make   97
    No Follow-Up = No Relationship = No Business
    Set a Contacting Goal
    Add a Minimum of Five People a Week

9. You Have to Have This to Succeed   105

10. A Special Message to Network Marketers   109
    Get Answers to These Questions Before Choosing a Network Marketing Company
    Contact Lists
    Transition to Business
    You Don't Know What Box They Are In
    Make Your Business System Dependent
    Hard Facts About Network Marketing

11. Online and Social Media Marketing   125
    Connecting Online
    Internet Resources You Can Use to Create Leads
    Article Directories
    More Lead Generators

12. Bonus Chapter   130
    The Secret to Attracting Leads
        Who Will Request You on Facebook
    Five Steps to Build a BIG Lead List Online

Putting It All Together   135
Disclaimer and Terms of Use   143

Foreword

One night in 2006 I attended a business networking event with about 100 people where I met Carl Randolph for the first time. Like most networking events, I had been mingling around introducing myself to others, exchanging pleasantries, and then moving on to the next person. When I met Carl, I suddenly lost interest in meeting anyone else because I was having such a great time talking with him. I don't know exactly what it was but because of his charisma and personality, I instantly liked him and wanted to be friends. I talked to him at least ten times longer than I did with anyone else that night. It was as if we were long lost brothers.

Meeting Carl is the only thing I remember about that night. Other than the fact that the event was put on by my best friend, Johnny Wimbrey, I totally forgot who the speakers were and can't remember any of the other people I met that night. Carl stood out, in a good way, as much as anyone I've met in my 19 years in business. So much so that four years later, when we had a chance to meet again, I remembered exactly who he was by name and even the conversation we had. I may not have known exactly what it was that caused him to make such a great impact on me at the time, but now after reading *How to Make Contacts and Win Friends* it's clear as day. The secret to Carl's like-ability from that first encounter is spelled out, step-by-step, in *How to Make Contacts and Win Friends*.

Since getting to work with Carl over the past two years, not only is he great with first impressions, he's even better once you really get to know him. Carl is one of the most genuine friends anyone could ask for. Of all the thousands of people I've worked with, Carl could easily be the poster boy for *How to Win Friends and Influence People*. If you've ever wanted to have a clear roadmap with an exact formula for being able to network like a pro, this book will spell it all out for you like no other book ever has. If this book were available when I started my career as an entrepreneur almost 20 years ago, I'm convinced it would have lessened my learning curve by many years. There are a lot of books written on people skills and networking but no other book shows you so specifically (literally word-for-word scripts) and comprehensively how to apply it for sales, network marketing, or any other career that requires you to contact others.

The book you now hold in your hands can become one of the most powerful tools you will ever have, if you will simply do as it suggests. So, read on and let Carl Randolph lead you through the process for *How to Make Contacts and Win Friends* like you never imagined.

Here's my best advice… **Don't just read this book – devour it!**

Matt Morris
International Speaker and Best-Selling
Author of *The Unemployed Millionaire*

Acknowledgments

I could write a whole chapter thanking all the people who have helped shape me into the person I am today, but here I would like to thank some special people who encouraged me in the writing of this book. Sheryl Randolph, the love of my life, I could not have written this book without your unconditional love and support. Every day I spend with you is a miracle day for me. I truly believe you are a miracle in my life. Thanks for all you do! It has not gone unnoticed. I just don't say thank you enough so—THANK YOU so much for all you do! There are simply no words I could write to let you know in full how I feel about you, so I will do my best to continue to show you. My love for you now is stronger than it was 37 years ago.

Carl (CJ), Aaron, and Chris Randolph thank you for believing in me and for writing some of the best notes and cards over the years to me. Your support and confidence in me is what every father would love to have from their children. CJ (creator of cramp prevention/relief http://OutLastElectrolytes.com) said, "It's about dang time you wrote a book!" There are not enough words to thank you three for all the love and encouragement you give me. I'm so proud of the men you have become. Keep striving! CJ, of all the women in this world, you found the perfect one for you in Lesley (Pinney) Randolph. I can't get enough of spending time with my grandsons, Gabe and Gideon. Love them for life! Aaron, you also made the absolute right choice when you married Breanna (Thomas) Randolph. Big congrats and success for you both! Ms. Donna Ali, I hope you know how proud I am of you and what joy you bring to my heart. Also, to my two beautiful granddaughters, Sinnead and Bianca Ali, stay focused on your dreams.

Carl Randolph

Thank you to the entire Randolph family, especially my mom who loved us all unconditionally (RIP)—I miss her so much—and my dad who did all he could to keep food on the table for eight of his sons. To the entire Christian family, thank you for all your love over the past 37 years. When I met your wonderful daughter, you all accepted me as I was and made me a part of your family. I could not imagine how different my life would be had I not married into your family.

Thanks to Matt and Rhonda Hopson, close friends for over 30 years for encouraging me to write a book and share it with the world; Tyrone Lister, for your constant words of wisdom and all your help pushing me to write: "Carl, the world needs to read your words"; Brandon Urbano for telling me over and over, "Carl, you need to write a book on contacting, and I will buy it."

It would be a grave disservice on my part not to mention these people. Each person has been there for me at a significant turning point in my life and I would like to personally thank Chris Thomas, Charles Prince, Craig Sweet, Johnny Wimbrey, Matt Morris, Loretta Calhoun, Demond Crump, Donald Bradley, and Roland Athouris, II.

Lastly, there are so many more people that have supported me - too many to mention here. However, I must say thank you to Tracy Day and Dr. Beverly Woodson Day, Jake and Val Willis, Dr. Rodney Bailey (RIP, my friend) and Gwen Bailey, and Henry and Aubree Stinson, III for your friendship through the years.

Introduction

It has always been natural for me to meet new people, and after many years of working with people in business, I realize that many of them struggle with this. I have a passion for helping others, so what better way to help others understand what to do OR what not to do, than to put what I have learned into a book. My wife nicknamed me **"The Encourager"** because she says I'm always encouraging others to stay focused on their dreams and never give up. If you knew certain techniques and had the opportunity to be prepared beforehand, your business or company, career or job—or whatever you do—would change overnight.

This book was put together primarily for people who are in business for themselves. However, the techniques can be used for anyone who wants to learn how to meet new people and build friendships.

If you are reading this book, that tells me you are looking to add new people to your existing network, whether you are already in a business, have a company, are looking to open a business, or just sell a product. Look no further! *How to Make Contacts and Win Friends* is a step-by-step guide and workbook to help you succeed.

The information you will have access to will literally change how you see meeting new people. The techniques here are all actual things I have done on a day-to-day basis for many, many years. This is not something that I just heard about. I have personally worked with individuals who were uncomfortable talking to people they didn't know. After coaching them through their particular situation, they are now meeting new people all the time. In Chapter 4, I will introduce you to a few people for whom meeting someone new was a challenge for one reason or another.

Not only do I explain how to meet new people, but I also provide leadership tips that will help you retain the relationships you make, which will help you to build your business or company.

In a perfect world you start a business by talking to family members and friends, they talk to other family members and friends, then those people talk to their family members and friends, and so on. The circle grows and you all make a lot of money. However, we don't live in a perfect world.

Therefore, to build a successful business or company, you will always need more customers, more clients, new members, or additional reps. The bottom line is sooner or later you will have to meet new people because you will realize you can't succeed without them.

Just like everything in life, the more you practice, the easier it will get and the better you will become. Therefore, it will become more natural to do.

I don't mind working, but I'd rather work smarter than harder. I'm thinking you would, too. I believe the techniques you will learn here will give you a better understanding of *How to Make Contacts and Win Friends*.

Get the Most Out of This Book

How to Make Contacts and Win Friends is not just a book to read. To get the most out of it, use it as a tool for learning, a guide, a base of knowledge. This book is setup in a way that gives you the opportunity to think as you read. It's educational, informational, as well as a workbook to write down your personal notes.

By adding your own personal notes as you read and reflect, you should retain more in this interactive format. Each time you refer back to your notes, add new ones to make the material more relatable to you personally as you grow and develop.

This book is full of examples, so when something pops into your head or triggers a thought as you are reading, jot it down right then and capture it on paper. There is space at the end of each chapter for additional notes. As you learn new techniques on how to meet new people, keep your book handy and add those new techniques, as well.

In Les Giblin's book, *Skill with People* (1968), he provides a table in which he describes "How we retain information." Giblin proposes that we learn:

10% of what we read

20% of what we hear

30% of what we see

50% of what we see and hear

70% of what we say as we talk

90% of what we say as we do a thing

So here's how you can get even more out of this book:

1. Create a desire to want to learn how to meet new people.
2. Take notes as you read.
3. Complete the questions at the end of the chapters.
4. Use what you learned immediately.
5. As you read, write down your thoughts that can be useful later.
6. Review your notes from time to time.
7. Be willing to step out of your comfort zone.
8. Have a "what's in it for me" mentality.

I hope you will follow the step-by-step instructions when asked, to help you become what I call an E-A-S-Y Method Specialist, which I will explain in Chapter 3.

Chapter 1

I Followed the System

When I started my business many years ago, I did exactly what my mentors told me to do. As times changed, I wanted to keep up with the new technology so I studied it and used what I learned. What I've come to realize is that both offline and online marketing work if you stay consistent. Everything works some of the time, but not all of the time. Listed below are all the things I have done over the years that have worked for me:

I refer to offline marketing as "Old School":

- Created a list of family and friends
- Employed the "three foot rule"
- Attended meetings, presentations, and functions
- Duplicated efforts
- Studied books and listened to tapes
- Edified leadership and team members
- Cold calling (some frozen calls)

I refer to online marketing as "New School":

- Built a list of potential clients
- Leads and auto responder
- Created personal blogs
- Submitted articles to hundreds of directories
- Sent "drip" emails to names on my list
- Teleconference calls
- Webinars
- Joined online groups (social media)
- Purchased online content
- Created lots of content
- Created YouTube videos

Marketing Trends

I'm aware that there is a new trend of marketing online. We call that the New School. I believe in using both old school and new school techniques. I don't want to limit myself to only marketing online because you never know whether the person who may be standing in front of you in line somewhere is the right person. I personally know several people who've made seven figures and have never placed an ad or prospected online. I'm not putting down anyone that doesn't cold contact or use the three foot rule. That's my opinion solely. I'm hoping it will make some sense to you once you read this book. Maybe you can use one of the techniques to help YOU or your employees to build a bigger business. Why would you ever leave money sitting on the table?

Change How You See Cold Marketing

Let's not think of making initial contacts as cold market contacting. Let's change that to contacting people you don't know yet or you have not met yet. It's funny how looking at something in a different way changes things. There are people out there waiting to meet you. You just have to open your mouth and say something. A stranger is a friend you have not met yet or a person you might be able to help. So, as of today, look at people you have not met yet as possible new friends. Write today's date here: Month ___ day ___ year _____.

We all have a sphere of influence; we all know perhaps 200, 700, or even more than 1,000 people. It's just a matter of recall. Most people only think of close friends and family members when they are asked to create a list of contacts to kick off their new company or business. We just don't think about ALL the people we have met over our lifetime, from first grade to today.

For those of you who don't have a perfect world scenario, I will provide several techniques on how to meet new people to add to your list for your company or business. So whether you are a very shy person or you have no problem meeting new people, you can still learn from reading this book.

The best advice I can give you is to go out each day and have fun. In the book *The Unemployed Millionaire: Escape the Rat Race, Fire Your Boss and Live Life on YOUR Terms!* (Wiley, 2009), Mr. Matt Morris writes about modeling: "I'm a big believer in a concept called modeling. Modeling is a simple formula that says to be hugely successful, find people who have experienced the results you want. Then figure out how they did it, do the exact same thing, and get similar if not identical results."

I have met thousands of people using my proven E-A-S-Y Method (see Chapter 3: How to Master the E-A-S-Y Method). Once mastered, it will have you meeting new people on a daily basis without getting stressed out as you're doing it. If I can do it, you can too! Just apply what you learn. Your life will never be the same once you see that people are just people and that without new people your business can never grow. The art of meeting people and finding a way to keep in touch with them will have a positive effect on your life, business, or company for years to come. Maybe, even for generations depending on the type of business or company you have.

We All Have Filters

We all have a filter, a wall, a shield, a built-in "What does this person want from me?" attitude. Lots of people have a barrier up in front of them. As you are talking to them for the first time, they may be wondering what you are up to.

People start making unconscious viewpoints about you right off the bat. People will make an immediate judgment about you, and you can't stop that; but you can help make that first encounter less stressful for both parties.

We all have a defense system based on our beliefs. People are afraid of rejection. We are told as we were growing up, "Don't talk to strangers" or "Be careful who you talk to." You must have had to raise your hand to speak in class at one point or another. Well, the result of that, for some kids, was that it created a fear of speaking unless they were spoken to.

In *How to Make Contacts and Win Friends,* you will learn how to build rapport with people you've just met. Your attitude is one of the first things people sense when they see you or speak to you. You will face many obstacles on your way to success, but who you become in the process might be more important than the money you make. You can only discover the new you by testing, revising, and refining new methods for yourself. You will learn who you really are, and the lessons you learn will last a life time.

People Are Looking

In today's economy, people are looking; people are hurting with all the layoffs and cutbacks. People might not say it, but they are more open to new ideas than ever before. Most people want to be successful, most people want to have money in the bank, and most people want their retirement to be there when they are ready for it. At the same time, it is always a good idea to have a plan B. The more you use the E-A-S-Y Method and make new contacts, the less likely you are to run out of people to talk to.

Just go out and be friendly and connect with people who connect with you. Let the conversation flow and don't try to force it. If a person is standoffish or not friendly, that's not your problem. Think of it this way, they're just missing out on having a good friend like you in their lives.

If they don't want to talk, leave them alone and move on. As you continue to meet new people, you will know when to back off or when you can continue the conversation. It may take time, but once you have it, you will be on the path to success—a path you never knew you could have found. Master the techniques in this book and your life will never be the same.

Just don't force the conversation; don't be pushy; and don't overlook the other person's reaction to you. If they don't seem to be connecting with you, that's totally OK; let them go. Make life fun, I say. Trying to make someone talk to you when they don't feel like it, is not making life fun!

It's All about Your Attitude

Get it into your mind that there is never a shortage of people—never. People are everywhere. No matter where you go, there are people there. Before I walk into a room or when I'm out and about, I already know I will meet someone new beforehand. I have the mindset and I assume that people will receive me, so I always know I will meet somebody because I tell myself I will. What you believe, you will receive.

The next time you walk through a restaurant (or building), walk like you own the place. Don't be arrogant but be confident and watch how people look at you. They will be thinking, who is that? It really works!

People who are great networkers somehow find a way to give more. In the end they will end up receiving more. Be a giver or become a giver. You will always reap what you sow, the good book says. Make talking to people fun. I always say, "Make life fun!" Get to a point where talking to someone you don't know is fun and you will be on your way to becoming an E-A-S-Y Method Specialist.

If you have a lot of success already, I'm pretty sure you didn't do it all by yourself. You had help, somewhere, sometime.

On the "Urban Faith" blog there is an article called: "Why Did Alex Haley Keep a Turtle's Picture in His Office?" Alex Haley, the author of *Roots: The Saga of an American Family* (Doubleday, 1976), kept a picture of a turtle in his office—a turtle sitting on a fence post. He said he kept it to remind him of a lesson he learned long ago: If you see a turtle on a fence post, you know he had some help getting there. Haley said, "Any time I start to think, 'Look how good I am,' I look at the turtle—me—and realize I did not get here by myself."

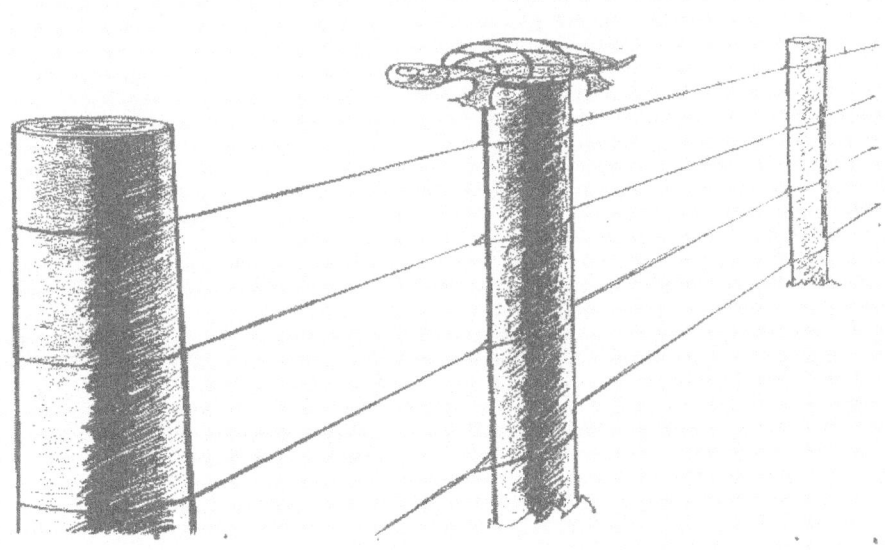

WOW! I'm a believer. That is so true in my life; and I'm willing to say that it's true in your life as well. You didn't get to where you are by yourself either.

I want this book to be a way for us to interact, and for you to think, so here's where I am asking you to write down some things that I think can help you become better at making new contacts and winning friends:

> **Key Points:**
> 1. Use both Old school and New school methods.
> 2. A stranger is a friend you have not met yet.
> 3. Go out and have fun...Make Life Fun!

Take this opportunity to write down a few things you've learned from this chapter:

Notes:

_____

_____

_____

_____

_____

_____

_____

Chapter 2

The Benefits of Networking

The first thing you must resolve in your mind is why you are doing what you're doing. Why are you networking? And what are the benefits? Are you ready to commit? Yes, commit! It will take commitment to build a customer base and build a business or company. You must first make up your mind that you are willing to commit to your dreams, whatever they may be.

The three magic words in networking are "leverage your time." If you are in network marketing, it is the only industry where the average person can leverage their time through other people's efforts. If you own your own business or you work for someone else, you still need new clients, customers, members, or reps. The bottom line is that you will always need new people. Most of us work for someone else but are not willing to work for ourselves. However, if you will commit to finding something you enjoy and work toward your dreams and goals, in the end it will be well worth it.

According to Wikipedia, the free online encyclopedia, networking is described like this:

> "Business networking is a socioeconomic business activity by which groups of like-minded business people

recognize, create, or act upon business opportunities. A business network is a type of business social network whose reason for existing is business activity. There are several prominent business networking organizations that create models of business networking activity that, when followed, allow the business person to build new business relationships and generate business opportunities at the same time.

1. Online Business Networking: Businesses are increasingly using business social networks as a means of growing their circle of business contacts and promoting themselves and their business online.

2. Face-to-Face Business Networking: Professionals who wish to leverage their business presentation skills with the urgency of physically being present attend general and exclusive business events.

3. General Business Networking: Before online business networking, there was and has always been, face-to-face business networking. "Schmoozing" or "rubbing elbows" are expressions used among professional business professionals for introducing and meeting one another in a business context, and establishing business rapport.

4. Networked Businesses: With business networking developing more business, many businesses now have this as a core part of their business strategy. Those businesses that have developed a strong network of business connections, suppliers, and

other businesses can be seen as Networked Businesses. They tend to source their business and their suppliers through the network of relationships they have in place."

Basically, networking is about meeting other people; and, based on what you are doing, you base your networking on the reasons why you need to meet new people.

Zig Zigler said, "You can get anything you want out of life if you just help enough people get what they want." In other words, if you help enough people pay their bills, you will get your bills paid. So, networking is also about seeing how you can help others. If you learn how to serve other people, you learn how to serve yourself in the process. People do business with people they like and trust. Learn all you can to get people to see you as genuinely likeable and trustworthy.

Dale Carnegie sums this up in his book *How to Win Friends & Influence People* (Pocket Books, 1998) in part 2, Chapter 6. In a nutshell, here are his six ways to make people like you:

1. Become genuinely interested in other people.
2. Smile.
3. Remember that a person's name is to that person the sweetest and most important sound in any language.
4. Be a good listener. Encourage others to talk about themselves.
5. Talk in terms of the other person's interests.
6. Make the other person feel important - and do it sincerely.

Learn how to be interested in others then you will build trust. People like to talk about themselves.

The Most Important Name

The most important name to a person is THEIR OWN! Sometimes I'm not good at pronouncing people's names, so I try to repeat their name several times as I'm talking to them.

Here's an example. You are a big sport fan and you see someone with your team's hat on (you can build an instant rapport most of the time). Here's how the conversation may go:

(You)   Hey man, I like the hat!
(Him)   Thanks!
(You)   My name is Carl.
(Him)   I'm Patrick.
(You)   Well, Patrick, I have been a big fan since I was a little kid. What about you?
(Him)   Not me, man, I have only been here for a few years and just recently became a fan.
(You)   Patrick, do you live near this area? I am from XYZ. (Continue the conversation.)

I used his name a few times to get it in my head and also to be sure I knew exactly how to pronounce it. (If the other person has a hard name to pronounce, ask them how to pronounce it.) How many times have you heard people say that they're terrible at remembering names? Well, they are right, if they tell themselves that. The subconscious mind said, "Yes, you are right. You can't remember names" (but that's another book...).

To help remember a person's name, relate it to someone else or to something. Here are some examples: For the name Ray, think of a sun Ray, or for Jordan, think of Jordan shoes. For Tony, I remember my cousin--I happen to have a cousin whose name is Tony. Practice repeating the person's name as you are talking and relate it to someone or something you can easily remember.

Les Giblin writes in the first chapter of *Skill with People*: "People are primarily interested in themselves, not in you! Putting this same thought another way – the other person is ten thousand times more interested in himself than he is in you."

Let Me Tell You a Little Story

A good friend calls you one night and says: "Hello _____, as you know, I'm friends with the governor and he and a few people have access to some rare diamonds. They have hidden five of those diamonds in a cave down near Moo's River in a certain section of the cave. He told me I could come and try to find the diamonds tomorrow night from 8:00 p.m. to 10:00 p.m. Here is the good part: He said I could bring four family members or good friends with me to find the diamonds. I'm not sure what you are doing tomorrow at 8:00 p.m., but can you make it?"

How many of you would have your shovel ready? Question: If this were a true story and you knew the governor personally, would you be there at 8:00 p.m. the next day and would you have four other people with you?

Circle one: YES or NO

If YES, why? Ask yourself why. The answer, first of all, is that you know the governor and you trust him. Second, there might be a good chance you could find one of those diamonds.

You are walking by diamonds every day and you are not saying a word to them. You have to look at your business, or whatever you are doing, like it is your diamond mine. You have people around you every day who could be your next best sale, customer, client, member, or rep.

Take a five-minute break and think about that story. Try to feel in your heart how you would really feel if that actually happened to you, and you found one of those diamonds. Try to capture the emotion of how you would react. Imagine the feeling you would have on the next call you make (if you are in a business or company right now).

> **Key Points:**
> 1. Commit to your dreams.
> 2. Leverage your time through other people.
> 3. Help others and you will help yourself.

Ok, welcome back! Your five-minute break is over! Now, let's start learning how to master the E-A-S-Y Method and start building relationships.

What did you get out of chapter2?

Notes:

_____

_____

Chapter 3

How to Master the E-A-S-Y Method

In this chapter I will explain what I do on a day-to-day basis to make contacts and win friends. Once you master it or at least get fairly good at it, you will be adding people to your list like magic! It's so easy I call it the E-A-S-Y Method.

E = Eye Contact	Make eye contact with the person.
A = Approachable	Does it look like it's a good time to approach this person?
S = Smile	Smile at them to see if they are friendly.
Y = Yes	Yes, you want to talk to them; or No, you don't want to talk to them.

Learning how to contact people is simple if you just focus on learning this method. Let me explain it in a little more detail. Many people don't feel comfortable talking to people they don't know. Remember, we already addressed the need to change the way you see new people in Chapter 1: They are friends you have not met yet.

The **"E"** is for Eye Contact. If you see someone you would like to talk to, approach that person and get close enough to make eye contact.

The **"A"** represents Approachable. If you feel the person or persons are approachable, once you get close enough, try to determine if this is a good time for them. They may have just gotten on the phone, or they might be distracted in some way. You will need to think fast about whether or not to start a conversation. So approachability is the key—follow your spirit, but don't force it. If it's a bad time for them, move on; you can re-approach them at a better time.

The **"S"** is for Smile. If you feel this is a good time, give them a slight smile and nod your head. There's no better device than a smile to catch someone's attention.

The **"Y"** is for Yes. You will know in your spirit if you want to go for it. If you're thinking, "I'm going to say something to them," then go ahead and say whatever comes to mind. (e.g., I like your shoes!) It might take a little time to master this but when you do, you will be adding people to your list faster than you know!

Most people will respond in a nice way and some will not. You are only looking for the easy ones.

Most people will smile back and some won't, but that's OK. You are not going to get them all, but once you master the E-A-S-Y Method, you will instinctively know who to talk to and who to leave alone. Just don't get frustrated! Keep practicing and I ensure you, someone will connect. Just keep going! Go for the easy ones. Sometimes people are having a bad day. Focus on making the easy contacts. To do this, say something as an ice breaker, basically to see if they are friendly or not.

I like sports, so when I go out I look for people with some type of Jersey: Cowboys, Packers, Saints, Longhorns, or any team. I might say:

"Did you see that throw by _____?"

"What a catch by _____!"

"Man, _____ ran like a train!"

Before you go out to meet people, get in front of a mirror and practice talking to yourself. You have to see yourself saying what you want to say when you meet someone new. People like to be around enthusiastic people and positive-energy types.

One of my favorite books is *From the Hood to Doing Good: From Adversity to Prosperity by the Choices You Make,* by Johnny Wimbrey (Westcom Press, 2003). He said: "The only people who never fail are those who never try. You must believe that you are a success before success can manifest itself in your life. It's literally impossible for you to believe it unless you say it first."

After you feel pretty confident and you have practiced a few times in the mirror, go to a place where you are comfortable, a place where you go often. Then, when you see someone you might want to talk to, think E-A-S-Y, and move close enough to make good eye contact. Yes, it's that easy: Eye contact – Approachable – Smile – Yes

Write it down on the back of a card and read it until you know it by heart. You will then remember what E-A-S-Y stands for in seconds. Take a deep breath and relax. The individual you see might be the one you are looking for, or they might not be, but you will never know if you don't speak. The person is not a stranger, just someone you have not met yet or someone you might be able to help.

Start by going to places where you enjoy doing things, such as football games, playing golf, jewelry shops, shopping, attending a club. Finding something in common is the most important part of meeting someone new if you are not in the habit of talking to new people. Something magical happens when you both have something in common or have had similar experiences.

Go out and make life fun! Look for the easy ones every day. When you use the E-A-S-Y Method, you will have plenty of people to talk to. You will have more friends than you can count if you are really interested in helping people.

Don't be afraid of people. They won't bite you!

People are sometimes in a bad mood. You could meet that same person the next day and they are as friendly as they can be. You may have just caught them at a bad time.

Just be natural when you are talking to people. Be yourself. Don't try to mimic someone else you've heard. Any time you try to be like someone else, you can't be the best you. You will always be a second or third best to someone else.

Remember the more you find in common with the person, the more comfortable they will feel about you and about connecting with you.

How to Build Rapport

Once you start to speak, resist being over anxious or jumping all over the person. They need to see that you are cool, calm, and confident.

How to Make Contacts and Win Friends

Don't try to overthink what you are going to say. Just go out and be friendly; be natural. Say what comes to your mind.

After you use the E-A-S-Y Method and you are talking to someone, keep these principles in mind to help build rapport. You are responsible for setting the tone, because within seconds they form an opinion of you based on your dress, your look, your tone of voice, and most importantly your attitude.

Be generally concerned for people. Speaking from your heart lets people see that you are a real person with feelings and that you have a heart for helping people. Wait for the right moment to make your approach, and then do it in a non-threatening way. If you feel good about it, go for it!

Remember, you are trying to make a friend and, if you do all the talking, you will not learn about them and who they are. You can't fake it! You need to be generally interested in them and sincere about listening to what they are saying.

Sometimes, nonverbal communication is as vital as verbal communication. If you are not making eye contact, have your arms crossed, or looking around while you are talking to someone, you are showing your disinterest. As you are talking, watch your tone and your volume because you want to create a bridge between you and them.

Make sure you are well groomed and your dress clothes are clean. Also, as you and the other person are talking, make sure you listen to what they are saying. Take mental notes in your head about what interests them. You will get better and better in time. Just keep talking to new people.

Be friendly but not too, too friendly. Avoid flattery. Never, ever flatter people! They will see right through it. If it's not true, don't say it.

Let the other person's opinions mean something. Let them feel they have some value. You may just need to nod your head and smile as they are talking. Do you want to make a friend? Do you want them to listen to you?

Don't compare people to other people. We are each unique in our own way so comparisons will only upset some people. Look to find what's good in them.

If, for some reason, you can't think of anything else to say and the conversation isn't flowing, you can always tell stories that encourage, uplift, or inspire. "Hey, Mike, did you hear…?" This will help you to build rapport and connect.

Never include the person you are talking to in a bad joke. As a matter of fact, stay away from using bad jokes. People like to feel comfortable, and most folks won't stay around if they don't feel relaxed. Watch and pay attention to their comfort level and be ready to try to make them feel at ease.

Be in a Hurry

Always be in a hurry. Leaders are always on their way to somewhere or just getting back from somewhere. However, this depends on your goal. If you are at a networking meeting and you want to meet x number of people, remember, it's not about you, it's all about them. You only have so much time to spend with each person. Be careful not to look around for the next person to talk to while you are still talking to someone else. Try to finish your conversation first.

Here are a few exit phrases to have ready at all times:

"Yes, (their name), we will definitely need to keep in touch with each other, but I see Joe and I need to touch base with him too."

"I hope you will forgive me, but I need to _____."

"Please excuse me; I have to make a call."

"Pardon me. I have to go to the bathroom."

"I was only stopping by but right now I have to get going."

"Man, I'm running late."

"Time just got away from me. I'm sorry, I have to go."

"Forgive me. I'm running late for my next appointment."

Exercise #1:

Write down two or three more exit phrases.

1. _____

2. _____

3. _____

Let's just say that you are talking to someone, and you figure out that this is not the type of person you would like to connect with. Use an exit phrase to get out of the conversation, don't waste your time. You can't get time back, so move on.

Do it in a way that it does not make it seem that you are trying to get out of the conversation. You will sometimes have to be a little patient and in a hurry at the same time.

Be Attentive to Gender and Other Dynamics

As you are talking to new people, keep in mind that there are different dynamics involved when you are talking to people of different ages, races, and genders.

Here are just a few examples:

Boy to Boy,

Boy to Girl,

Man to Woman,

Man to Man,

Young Man to Older Man,

Young Man to Older Woman,

White to Black,

Hispanic to White, etc.

So, keep these dynamics in mind as you are talking to people. You might not have a problem with any of the above dynamics, but you may need to be ready to change up your conversation if you need to. Pay special attention to the boy-girl and man-woman dynamics. Mention your wife or girlfriend or husband or boyfriend if you are talking to a single person of the opposite gender.

Here are a few more examples:

If you are a young man and the other person is an older man, let him know you are connected with other people older than you so he can relate.

If you are talking to a woman and you are a married man, mention your wife within the first few seconds of the conversation. This shows her that you are not trying to come on to her.

Do's and Don'ts

Let's start with the Don'ts. Here are a few Don'ts to keep in mind as you are talking to people (others mentioned throughout the book):

- Don't stare them down.
- Don't hog the conversation and do all the talking.
- Don't joke about them or other people.
- Don't make it all about you.
- Don't ask questions, one right after another.
- Don't make up things you know nothing about.
- Don't force the conversation.
- Don't be pushy.
- Don't cut people off.
- Don't flatter people; be honest.
- Don't ask really personal questions right up front.
- Don't cross your arms or legs (unless they have theirs crossed).

Here are a few Do's to keep in mind when you are talking to people:

- Do let them talk about themselves.
- Do add to the conversation.
- Do tell them a little about you.
- Do laugh doing the conversation when the time is right.
- Do say something positive about other people.
- Do give a compliment if it is warranted.
- Do give people their space.
- Do keep the conversation upbeat, and avoid dead airtime.
- Do think before you answer.
- Do look in their eyes from time to time.
- Do smile doing the conversation when the time is right.
- Do make them feel like you are old friends just talking.
- Do repeat their name to remember it.

Over the years, I've been guilty of doing most of the things I say not to do. So, I'm writing from a personal point of view. Why am I doing this? I've put together this list of Do's and Don'ts so you will not make the same mistakes I did; so you can get off to a much better start. Use my experience to your advantage and don't do what I did wrong.

You will find as you continue to use the E-A-S-Y Method, that it will become such a part of you over time, soon you won't even have to think to use it! Anyone can learn the skills that it takes to meet someone new. You just have to practice getting comfortable with your approach.

How to Make Contacts and Win Friends

> **Key Points:**
> 1. You must believe that you are a success.
> 2. Start by going to places you enjoy going.
> 3. Get the easy ones.

What was the most important lesson you learned from this chapter?

Notes:

_____
_____
_____
_____
_____
_____
_____
_____
_____
_____

Chapter 4

The H-C-Q-C Process

I honestly believe that I can help anyone who dreams of meeting new people or who desires to make new contacts, win friends, and potentially increase the size of their business or company. There is a method I called The H-C-Q-C Process. It has worked for many, many people over the years. It doesn't matter how afraid you might be of meeting people, the process works if you have any passion or desire to meet new people. If you are a very shy person, you just don't know where to start, or you may over analyze and talk yourself out of meeting new people, then you are not alone.

I would like to introduce you to three people whom I've helped overcome those challenges and set on a path to successfully talk to people:

> Ms. Lynette Victor from Austin, Texas – When it came to talking to people, she would overanalyze what she wanted to say and talk her way out of making the contact.

Mrs. Lashette Griffeth from Richardson, Texas – When I met her, she was as quiet as a church mouse—I mean she was very, very shy!

Mr. Brandon Urbano from Dallas, Texas – Brandon wanted to break out of his shell—he just needed some guidance.

For those people who for some reason just can't start off using the E-A-S-Y Method, don't fear because I have a proven four-step process that I put together many years ago called the H-C-Q-C Process. If you follow this process, I believe anyone can learn how to talk to new people in their own time and within their own comfort zone.

H = Hi or **H**ello
C = Comment
Q = Question
C = Connect

A Passionate Goal

First, I ask the person how serious they are about accomplishing their dreams or goals. If they are serious, I have them write down those dreams or goals. Then I pick one that they are passionate about, and I tell them that they have to make their goal bigger than their fear of talking to people.

Here is the process I have them focus on:

I have them take the time to develop a strong WHY to explain their dreams and goals. Once we have established one major goal and they are ready, I send them through the process. Some take longer than others, but anyone can accomplish this process.

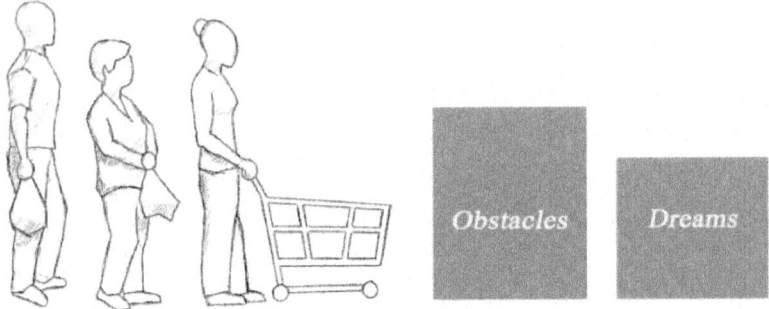

You will have obstacles. We all have them in our lives. You can't get away from things that happen. All you can do is control how you react to what happens. You must make your dreams, your why, your goals bigger than your obstacles. Picture yourself in a store, and there is someone (a potential superstar) standing right in front of you. If your dream is not big enough, you won't say anything.

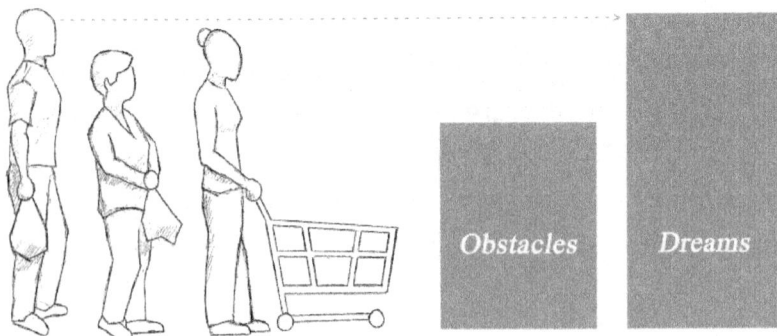

You can have the same obstacles in life, but if your dreams are bigger than your obstacles and you stay focused, you can see them. If you can see them, you can achieve them. Now, picture yourself in the same store, and because your dreams are bigger than your obstacles, you will say something. Now you could potentially have a superstar connected with your business or in your company with you.

How the H-C-Q-C Process Works

First, go to a place where you enjoy going. Choose a place where you are most comfortable and where there are people.

For the next three days, just look at three people each day with a slight smile, and only say "Hi" or "Hello." That's all! Yes, just "Hi" or "Hello," and nothing else. That is all I want you to do.

If you want to use the four-step H-C-Q-C Process, start tomorrow and keep a record. Hold yourself to the process by keeping a simple chart and using it right from day one.

Day One:

Today's date is _____.

Step #1. "Hi" or "Hello"

For the next three days, I want you to just look at three people you don't know and with a slight smile, just say "Hi" or "Hello." That's ALL. Nothing else.

Did you smile and say "Hi" or "Hello"?

(Circle yes or no)

1. Person #1   yes or no
2. Person #2   yes or no
3. Person #3   yes or no

It might take you a few days to get comfortable even saying "Hi or Hello". So proceed at your own pace and at your own comfort level. Once you feel good just saying "Hi" or "Hello" to new people, move on to step #2.

Step #2. Comment

This is the same as step #1 except this time say "Hi" or "Hello" and add one comment.

Today's date is _____.

"Hi, it's cold out there today!" or

"Hello, what a nice day it is today!"

Did you smile, say "Hi" or "Hello," and make a comment?

(Circle yes or no)

1. Person #1   yes or no
2. Person #2   yes or no
3. Person #3   yes or no

Remember, do this until you get comfortable saying "Hi" or "Hello" and adding a comment. Proceed at your own pace and at your

How to Make Contacts and Win Friends

own comfort level. Once you feel pretty good saying "Hi" or "Hello" and making a comment to new people, move on to step #3.

Step #3. Question

Add a question: "Hi" or "Hello," comment, and question.

Today's date is _____.

"Hi, I like your shoes!"
> (They answer), "Are you from around here?"

"Hi, it's a nice day today!"
> (They answer), "You look familiar. Did you go to ABC school?"

"Hello, man the traffic was bad today!"
> (They answer), "Yeah, but I'm still so glad to get out and about. Have you been working here long?"

Write down three other comments that come to your mind:

1. _____
2. _____
3. _____

Now write down three more questions that come to your mind:

1. _____
2. _____
3. _____

Do this over and over and over until you feel comfortable. It might feel a little awkward at first, but if you just keep your why or your dreams in the forefront of your mind, you will get better and better each day. Before you know it, you will be a pro!

I say, "Look for the easy ones." If someone seems mad or in a bad mood, you just keep moving. Don't let people get to you.

If you have the type of business or company where you need to meet new people or to recruit, then you will need to get their contact information.

Once you feel comfortable with step #3 and it starts getting easier and easier, you will need to move to step #4 and start to connect with them.

Hi or **H**ello – **C**omment – **Q**uestion – **C**onnect:

Step #4. Connect

To move on to the connection step, you will need to get their contact information or find a way to keep in touch. You will need to have a little more conversation to see if you both feel comfortable enough to exchange information. Once you make it to this part, use some of the Do's and Don'ts in Chapter 3, How to Master the E-A-S-Y Method.

Start with your dreams, your WHY, and write them down on a card or something to look at. Go to a place where you feel you can hold a conversation with another person if they were to ask you questions.

How to Make Contacts and Win Friends

Don't go out trying to get people into your business or your company or trying to make a sale immediately. Just go out and be friendly. Go out to make a friend and if it leads to business, then great!

Exchange Contact Information

When you first start, don't ask for their number directly. As you are talking and it feels like a good fit, you might say something like:

"I enjoyed talking to you. Let's exchange contact information and keep in touch."

"_____, I really enjoyed talking to you, and I would like us to keep in touch. Let's exchange contact information and I will give you a call later this week."

"_____, I have a few friends I believe you would like to meet. You remind me of them. How can I get in touch with you?"

"_____, my business partner, is always looking for sharp people to talk to, and I am sure she would not mind talking to you. What is the best way I can contact you?"

This is my special one. I have used this one and I have gotten a number every time:

"Hey _____, I don't have a card on me . . .Oh, you know what, let's use technology; let me just text you my info."

Pay close attention here on how I get a number. It's got to be a smooth flow:

"Hey ____, I don't have a card on me . . .Oh, you know what, let's use technology; let me just text you my info. What's a good number I can text you my information?"

Make sure you do it all together in one statement without pausing. Don't say:

"Hey ____, I don't have a card on me . . .Oh, you know what, let's just use technology . . . (Pause) . . . What's a good number I can text you my information?"

Or

"Hey ____, I don't have a card on me . . .Oh, you know what, let's just use technology . . . (Pause) . . . can I get your number?"

You can also see that I didn't ask if I can have their number. I asked what is a good number to text them my information. Based on their comfort level, they will give you the number they feel most comfortable giving.

If you combine the E-A-S-Y Method with the H-C-Q-C Process, you will be well on your way to becoming someone to be reckoned with, a real superstar, and real soon. Let me be the first one to congratulate you.

I believe anyone (and I mean anyone) can be taught how to meet new people if they learn the step-by-step H-C-Q-C Process.

If shy and introverted people can make contacts and win friends using this method, so can you. Let me introduce you to Lashette. She was so shy—and yes, I did say "was." Now, however, she can hold her own. I will let Lashette explain in her own words.

Lashette Griffieth

During my years on this earth, I've always been the shy one. I didn't talk a lot, I was very quiet. A year or so ago I was introduced to a wonderful business concept. I mean it was great, and I wanted to do my best to make it work, but there was one problem... I was scared to talk to people. When I say scared I mean I didn't know how to spark a conversation with people I didn't know. I guess I was too worried about how they would look at me or if I would be able to answer questions the correct way. I was also afraid of rejection.

One day, I was invited to a friend's house and I met a man named Carl. He was very outgoing and wasn't afraid to talk in front of anyone. I was thinking to myself, I wish I could be like him, outgoing and not afraid. I finally had a chance to speak with him and he laid out a plan to push me forward. He has helped me find that passion and burning desire to WIN, and I really appreciate him for taking the time to help me. I decided to do this for my family.

I especially appreciate Lashette's words because they will help empower someone else who is shy to have the courage to go out and use the H-C-Q-C Process. I'm so proud of her because she also realizes that family is very, very important. Now let's hear from another young lady, Lynette, also in her own words, how the H-C-Q-C Process helped her get pointed in the right direction.

Lynette Victor

I attended a conference in Las Vegas in April 2012. So many aspiring entrepreneurs were there. I knew that I was in the right place at the right time. I've always been told that you need to connect with the people that have the talent that you want or need to develop yourself in life. For the past 13 years, I sat behind a desk only speaking to people calling in or arriving for meetings with office executives. Life was quite different for me in that "safe place." There was no need to make the first move to introduce myself. Most guests already knew who I was by association.

However, that conference I attended opened my eyes to so much more in life. As I was walking down a corridor and I passed this gentleman and his wife. His presence was unique and genuine. He was friendly and you could tell by his conversations that he never met a stranger. I was amazed. All this little ex-federal government worker could think was, "Where in the heck did I put my MoJo?" This guy has exactly what I've been in search of! Needless to say, I got the nerve up to finally stop him and his wife to exchange numbers. That was the first time I met Carl and Sheryl Randolph.

How to Make Contacts and Win Friends

In speaking with Carl a number of times after, I finally decided to ask him to mentor me in finding quality people and building strategic relationships to advance as an entrepreneur. By this time in my new career, I had already spoken to close friends and family. I shared with Carl my hesitancy to approach new people. He told me that if I meet him halfway, he would meet me halfway. Meaning, I had to do my part to grow out of the shell I found myself in. My first assignment was to simply go out and say hello to people. Don't talk about business, he said. Just say "Hello." I tried it and I experienced a communication block that made me uncomfortable around new people. When I attempted to approach them, I'd chicken out. That wasn't easy to admit. After all, I never had this problem before. Going into business changed my perspective for some reason.

In sharing this with Carl, he told me that I'm overanalyzing what to say and how to say it. So, I went out a second time and tried it again. Once I mastered "Hello," Carl then told me that my second assignment was to go out and say "Hello, it's a nice today!" and to make some type of small talk. Just go out and gain confidence in having small talk (while holding at bay, the script running fiercely in my head). That had been the biggest challenge of my life, but the barrier finally broke. I don't fear speaking to new people now and my quality of people to do business with has substantially improved. I'm still a work in progress. However, thanks to Carl Randolph, I'm progressively growing in the right direction now.

I tell people that, like Lynette, there are many people who overthink what they are going to say but, if they continue to progress at their own comfort level, it will get easier and easier as they keep trying.

The third person whose words I want to share with you is Brandon. He is one of the friendliest people I have ever met. Going out to meet new people, however, was something he had a challenge with.

Brandon Urbano

Prior to meeting Carl Randolph, I was a very introverted individual. Meeting people was always a challenge for me and I tended to shy away from confrontation. Part of it was that I lacked the confidence and knowledge of what to say and do on the first encounter. Although having leadership experience in the Army as an Officer, I often found myself shying away from many social functions or "Officer Calls," which were basically networking events designed to assist in the advancement of one's career by placing the officer in front of a Potential Future Commander.

Carl showed me what to say and do during the first contact to make a favorable impression and how to properly win friends and increase my network. The hardest thing for one to do is to put his/her ego in check and allow someone else to mentor and train him/her. I realized quickly by watching Carl in the field, that he was one to emulate. I remember him greeting a man in the gas station. He never said, "Watch this," but I knew right away that he was teaching me by showing me what to do. Carl makes meeting people so effortless. I never considered that I could become as comfortable with meeting people that I am now only one year after working with Carl.

At a company-sponsored function, Carl started to share his knowledge immediately. Whether it was at the gas station or at a coffee shop, he would simply walk up to someone and begin a conversation. This is the way he first showed me that it was possible, that it was not simply about the making of the contact but more of just being friendly, not trying to "Get that one!" At the function he said, "I don't want you to go out and make contacts, I just want you to go out and extend your hand and say, 'Hi, I'm Brandon.'" I tried this with 10 random people, male and female, and I was surprised at the results. I was able to meet and expand my network with this simple teaching.

I remember what meeting people was like prior to Carl. I would attempt to make conversation with subjects I knew little about or was not passionate about. The conversation always seemed to be forced and never comfortable. One year later, I am able to meet others and understand the power of the pre-impression prior to the first impression. I now know people from around the world and my personal circle has been expanded. This is all thanks to Carl, and his teaching. The best part of knowing how to meet and talk to others is that, like a bike, once learned it's not easily forgotten. I am now considered to be an extroverted individual. When compared to my personality a year ago, some come away surprised and find it hard to believe that I was ever introverted at all.

I congratulate Brandon, and people like him. It does my heart good when I see that they overcome their lack of confidence by using the techniques I spell out in this book. And I say, "Keep going!"

To help build confidence, you can pair up with someone or go out in small groups to support each other. One person might be more relatable than the other. Just find your balance and keep on refining it until you don't even realize you are doing it. It will just come natural. You can do it! You already have what it takes to do it!

Congratulations! You are on your way to becoming an E-A-S-Y Method Specialist.

Key Points:
1. Write down a goal that you are passionate about.
2. Make your goal stronger than your fear.
3. Go out and be friendly.

Write down a reason why you have a problem approaching someone you don't know and what you can do to change that.

Notes:

_____

_____

_____

Chapter 5

Make Contacts and Build Relationships

In Chapter 1 of Dale Carnegie's book, *How to Win Friends and Influence People*, he writes: "If you want to gather honey, don't kick over the beehive." He mentions his first principle: "Don't criticize, condemn or complain." Use this principle when you are connecting online as well.

Common interest is the key to meeting people fast, because you will be able to relate on the same subject. Having a common interest makes it easy to start a conversation. The more you understand the subject you and the person are discussing, the easier it is to connect and exchange numbers. It's been said so many times that people do business with people they like and trust. So you need to learn how to build trust fast and get the other person to like you. Start off by making the best impression you can.

Watch Your Personal Hygiene

Being attentive to your personal hygiene is very important. When you are out, always try to look your best. I'm not saying you have to wear a suit and tie all of the time, or go out and buy all new clothes; what I'm saying is just be neat and clean. Be the best you can be.

Here are some things to avoid:

- Dirty hands and finger nails
- Torn clothes
- Holes in your shoes
- Hair not combed
- Food between your teeth
- Dirty face (unless you just got off work)
- Wrinkled clothes
- Body odor
- Offensive picture on your shirt
- Facial hair not trimmed or neat

Good personal hygiene is a must, and I know this is just common sense, but sometimes people just don't think. You would be surprised how many people don't think about how their breath smells after certain meals. After you eat something like onions or garlic, make sure that your breath is fresh when you're meeting people. Keep some mints or gum with you. It will be hard to meet someone new if they are being repelled from you by your breath. Just be cautious as you are talking to people.

My message here is that you want to make your Pre-Impression (discussed in next section) the best one you can. You need to make it as pleasant as possible, because you have NO idea what that person is thinking of you. So, minimize anything that could possibly turn off that person and keep them from meeting you. Keep in mind that you always need to do your part. However, you still will not get them all, no matter how nice you smell or look or talk, but that's OK... NEXT!

PI: The Pre-Impression

You ask, "What do you mean by PI?" Imagine, if you will, the impression before the first impression. That's what I call the Pre-Impression (PI). It is in our nature that most of us start judging people before we even meet them. When we see someone, we automatically start to size them up...how they look...what they're wearing, etc.

Let me give you an example. You're at a business luncheon. Ninety-eight percent of the men are wearing a suit and tie, and the other two percent have on jackets and slacks. You don't know Bob, but Bob walks in wearing shorts and a pullover shirt. You think to yourself, "Wow, he looks out of place. Why would he come dressed like that?" Most people would probably judge Bob simply because of the way he's dressed. That's what I call PI.

You have no idea why Bob is underdressed at that particular luncheon. At the break, Mike introduces Bob to you and Bob immediately says, "I apologize for the way I'm dressed, but I'm just visiting from out of town and Mike insisted I stop by this luncheon. He said no one would be concerned with my shorts, but had I known everyone would be dressed up, I probably would have never stopped in." Now your impression of Bob will be a little different because he explained why he was dressed that way.

First Impression

When you're out and about, you want to make a good first impression, because perception is real. People are judging you before they even meet you (PI).

So here are a few steps to take to make a good first impression:

1. Look good and dress nice.
2. Be friendly.
3. Smile.
4. Be confident but not arrogant.
5. Be excited but not "over the top" excited.
6. Have a good handshake and look people in the eye.
7. Be interested, not interesting.
8. Speak first and listen for each person's name. Use their name three times in the conversation so you can remember it.

Give Compliments

Learn how to give compliments. Here are a few simple ones you can use: "That's a nice car." – "I love your shoes." – "Those earrings are off the chain!" - "I like that hat." – "Those are some cute kids." – "That is an awesome football jersey." – "Do you mind if I ask where you got that coat; it's very cool." Giving sincere compliments is a great way to start a conversation when you're using the E-A-S-Y Method.

Say something good about another friend you know who is in the same field. Be uplifting and happy, and try to keep the conversation positive. If something negative does come up, change the subject or speak to it quickly and get the conversation back in positive territory. You want to show empathy, but don't stay there too long; just don't dwell on negative things.

Build Trust

The best way to build trust is to listen to what others are saying. Let them feel they can trust you because you listened and tried to help. Here's an example: "Hello, my name is Mike Brown." (Extend your hand to shake their hand. Most people will reply with their name.) "Well, Donnie, it's so nice to meet you."

During the conversation you find out that Donnie enjoys golfing, and your brother-in-law is a golfer as well. Your brother-in-law was telling you about a special club he ordered off of the internet and so you convey this to Donnie. Let Donnie know that you'll let him know where your brother-in-law got the club. In other words, you want to find some type of *common ground* with each person you meet. You want to ask questions, but *don't* make it seem as if you're interrogating them. You want to offer some of your life to the conversation by telling them a little about yourself as well.

Here are a few more don'ts to keep in mind when you meet someone:

- Don't always be the one to have the better story.
- Don't talk on and on and on.
- Don't ever put down their competitors.
- Don't be the "one-upmanship" type.
- Don't argue. You may have a different opinion, and that's OK, but don't get into an argument.
- Don't think you know everything.
- Don't look like you are preoccupied with other things as you are talking.
- Don't act unfriendly or like you are upset.

Here is the one don't I had to learn the hard way. Don't try to change people. Once you meet someone and you start to build a friendship, don't try to change that person unless they personally ask you to help them change something. You can't change people unless they want to change themselves. If you are trying to change someone over to the way you think, and they are not hearing it, do yourself a BIG favor and STOP!

I had a business card in my wallet for many years that read, "I'm so busy trying to change Carl, that I don't have time to change anyone else." Whatever business or company you are in, spend your time working on you and getting better at what you do. Then you will attract others. You be the one who sets the example, and people will want to know what you are doing.

If you say something and find out it's not true, be ready and willing to say: "I heard that but I must be wrong; maybe my information was bad. Sorry, let me go back and check my source." or "I thought I heard that from someone but maybe they were wrong."

I know this is all common sense, but sometimes we want to impress people by how much we know or how smart we are, but that's not what it's all about. It's about learning how to make new friends and grow your business or company. It's OK to admit you're wrong: "I saw that on a YouTube video and maybe it was wrong. Maybe it was just a prank or something." In other words, you don't have to be right all the time. Do you want to be right or make a friend?

Les Giblin writes in Chapter 2 of *Skill with People*: "Take these four words out of your vocabulary, 'I, me, my, mine.'" He writes, "Substitute for those four words, one word, the most powerful word spoken by the human tongue—'YOU.'"

How to Make Contacts and Win Friends

Yes, the word "YOU" is much more powerful than the word "I" when you are talking to people. Try to get others to talk about themselves (the sweetest name to them is their own). If you show that other person you are more interested in them and what they are saying, you will be well received. However, if you talk about how interesting you are and do not give them the opportunity to talk about themselves, you may not be well received at all. So, change your total perspective about meeting new people and adopt this philosophy: "I'm going to be more interested in others and talk to the ones who are friendly." By doing this you will be more successful.

In a conversation, make sure you do what I call "the give and take." In other words, you give to the conversation. You tell them a little about yourself but keep the conversation on them. People are more interested in themselves. Make sure you're not interrogating them with one question after another.

Here's an example of the wrong way: "Hello, my name is Jay Crosby." (He says his name is Bobby.) "Hello, Bobby, it's nice to meet you. Do you live around here? Do you have any kids? What type of work do you do? What company are you with? How long have you been working there?"

Here's a better way to handle that conversation. "Hello, my name is Jay Crosby." (He says his name is Bobby.) "Hello Bobby, it's nice to meet you. Do you live in the area?" (He answers.) "Well Bobby, I have a brother that lives right in that area and I am in that area a few times a year, but I live in Dallas. Do you have any little ones yet?" (He answers.) "Two boys, great! We have three boys and my wife says that's it! We'll just have to wait for the granddaughter if I want that girl. I'm working in the computer field, Bobby. What type of profession are you in?"

I think you get the flow of give and take. You give, and then you take from the conversation, but make sure you take more than you give.

Try to find out what's important to them—what they like, what they want from life, their hobbies. Be an active listener rather than a passive hearer. Now I must admit, this one is hard for me, and I work on this one daily. Try not to think about your next contact or some unrelated issue when you should be listening.

Sorry golfers, I've never played, but if the person I'm talking to plays golf, we will talk about playing golf. "Why?" Because I want to be interested and relate to them. The more relatable you are to them, the more comfortable they will be with you.

So I want you to keep this in mind. After your next conversation, ask yourself if you know more about them or did they learn more about you?

Be interested in the other person. Nod your head and say: "I see what you are saying," or "I see what you mean." You want to be a good listener, but don't stare down the other person to try to make it look like you are hearing every word they are saying. You want to look at them about 70 to 80 percent of the time. Share information about yourself. Learn a few stories you can always bring up if the conversation is not going anywhere.

Some people can read your face. They can tell how you really feel by the way you look and how you react as they are talking to you. Watch your facial expressions. Some people can't help it, but their face says it all. If you are trying to make a connection and you are all frowned up or your face is saying something different than what you are saying, people will pick up on it. Smile and be friendly!

Everyone has their own personal space, so be careful not to invade it when you are talking to people. I was not a big hugger at all, and I didn't care for men to hug me. My dad was not a big hugger when I was growing up, so I wasn't used to that. I have lightened up a lot since then.

As I said, we all have our own personal space and if you invade that space, you can turn people off. Hugging someone you just met, getting right in their face or holding their spouse's hand too long when you meet them can be a big turn off.

Based on the conversation and your comfort zone, ask for the contact information and make the connection. I have learned over the years that you can determine how much they trust or don't trust you based on what information they give you. For example, if you say, "Let's exchange information," and they only give you their email address, they may not trust you. If they give you their personal cell number, that shows a little more trust. If they give you their personal cell number, work number and email address, they really trust you based on your conversation.

At the right time, repeat something they said earlier in the conversation. For instance: "It was great meeting you, and I do hope you get the new position you were talking about earlier. By the way, let's keep in touch so you can let me know how it worked out." This lets them know you were listening to what they were saying. Be interested in them. Don't take it personal if they don't give you their number or information. You never want to come across as mad, upset, or unpleasant in the conversation.

Write down three other connection statements you can use to stay in touch and get their information.

1._____

2._____

3._____

I know you are probably thinking, I bought this book to learn from him and he's asking me to work. Yes, I'm asking so we can interact and so I can get you to think along with me. Your connection phrases will mean a lot more to you than my connection phrases.

I'm asking you to work because you will feel much more comfortable with what *you* say, not with what *I* say. So, yes, I'm asking you to work because once you master the E-A-S-Y Method, the sky will be the limit for you and your business or company. (As a matter of fact, there is no limit!) If your business or company needs people and you have the skill to meet new people, who can hold you back? NO-ONE but you!

Connect with the Person

You are always in control. Find a way to keep yourself in front of people if not every day, a few times a week. Just be open, and be ready to contact new people.

The more you can connect with a person, the easier it is to get back with that person. You always want to leave on a positive note. (Example) "Donnie, I really enjoyed talking to you. I will talk to my brother-in-law and get back with you, but I see someone I need to talk to before I leave here."

You can connect with all the people in the world and build great friendships, but don't be a situational type of person, be a person of principle. You ask, "So what do you mean, Carl?" Here's what I mean: As you are connecting and building a relationship with people, be a person of principle as you talk to them. Be consistent in what you say. For example, you told one person how you feel about a certain situation yesterday, and then today you tell another person in the same situation just the opposite, or something completely different from what you told the other person yesterday. Somewhere down the line, they may meet and exchange what you told them. So, just be a person of principle and people will learn to trust you. If you are a situational type of person, sooner or later it will catch up to you, especially if you are in the same business or company as both people.

Keep in mind, you are looking for individuals you can connect with; and basically think of the others as practice. You are just practicing with some of them until you find the right one. It's all in how you look at it. You could say: "I used the E-A-S-Y Method on five people today, but I only made one connection." Well, first of all, you would have gotten zero connections had you not talked to five, and second, what if that one person becomes a superstar in what you are doing? Just go through the numbers and the people you are supposed to connect with will connect with you.

For the ones you choose not to connect with, always have an exit strategy ready. Create a few exit statements for yourself that you're comfortable with. If you start to talk to someone and you feel like you don't care for them, get out of the conversation and move on. Don't let people take up your time. You're in charge of yourself, so stay in control. Don't prejudge, but you know who you are looking for.

Be professional when meeting people. Don't look at your cell every few minutes. If you do get a call and it's important, say: "Excuse me. I really have to take this call. I'll be right back." Be open when you are talking to someone; in other words, don't have your hands in your pocket or be moving all around in your chair as you are talking.

It is very important to take note of your body language. Introduce yourself and speak clearly and sufficiently loud with good eye contact and a firm handshake. Be positive and add to the conversation, but don't take it over; put your ego aside for a few minutes. Also, be aware of the other person's body language and how they are reacting to you as you are talking to them. Don't look like you need this person. They can feel it if you are acting like a needy person. You don't need everyone, you just need the right ones.

Sometime you might have to ask some people questions in a subtle way versus being direct. Some people don't like you to ask them direct questions. As you are talking to them, if you feel they are like that, ask your questions a little different, more indirectly:

> "Oh, are you and the Mrs.' going on vacation anytime soon?" instead of "Are you married?"
>
> "Do you have any little ones yet?" versus "How many kids do you have?"
>
> "Do you live in the area?" and not "Where do you live?"

"I try to hit the ball a few times a week, what about you?" rather than **"**Do you play golf?"

"My favorite hobby is XYZ, do you have one?" as opposed to **"**Do you have a hobby?"

In each instance it's basically the same question, just phrased a little differently.

Here are a few examples of the types of people you will run into; just be ready for them. Learn to adapt, and be ready with an exit statement.

They seem a little reserved.

They are not friendly at all.

They are friendly but don't really say much.

They are very friendly and talk the whole time.

They are too friendly.

They are very cold and closed minded individuals.

Here is what you are looking for:

They enjoy your conversation and want to keep in touch.

They enjoy your conversation and want to find out more about what you are doing.

Focusing on the person

Make sure when you're talking to a person that you're focusing on what they're saying and you're not constantly looking around the room trying to see who you're going to talk to next. You want to make your prospect feel that he/she is the most important person in the room. (He or she just might be!)

One of my biggest challenges (and I am still working on it!) is not to get distracted by other people around me. Depending on my mood for that day, I would be ready to move on to the next person fast once I got their number.

My wife, on the other hand, finds it very hard to break away from a person while they are talking. Many times, by the time I would have 10 numbers, she might have one or two. However, I must admit, some of the time her two contacts turn out to be better connections than my 10. She takes the time to really get to know that person. (She is a yellow, green—which I will explain in the next chapter.)

Try to help out if you can. Based on the conversation you have with the prospect, if you have access to or are aware of an article with any information that could help that person you are talking to, try to help them out. Send them a letter or an email with the magazine article attached. Help solve people's problems if you can.

If you have another business friend with whom you feel this person would be a good match, refer them (but be careful here). You might say, "My friend, John, would love to meet you. You both have so much in common!"

You Will Experience Rejection

You will experience rejection, so be ready for it. You will need to develop your own method for how to handle it, because it will happen; it's a part of life. We have all been rejected at one time or another in our lives.

Sometimes you catch people at the wrong time. Maybe they just got laid off: or they had an argument with someone or maybe they got some bad news. Perhaps a family member was sick or they just broke it off with someone. Maybe they are just an unfriendly person—you can't let it bother you. Keep your dreams on a card and look at that card three times a day. You have to come up with a way to let it just run off your back like water off a duck's back. Here's what I say to myself: "They are having a bad day, and I interrupted it." I just think "NEXT!"

Don't Be So Quick to Hand Out Your Business Card

Don't be so quick to just hand out your business card and move on to the next person. You want to spend a little time talking—but not all day. You will get better at gauging your time per person as you keep doing it, but try not to be the first one to hand your card out during the conversation.

Here's an example: "Well, Donnie, it was great talking to you, and I will see if I can find out where my brother-in-law ordered that golf club. What's the best way that I can get back with you?"

Based on the information he gives, you will know how comfortable he feels with you and how much he trusts you.

- Email address = little trust
- Cell # = Higher trust
- Cell/work # and email address = Highest trust (You won him/her over!)

If you are meeting people and you don't get their contact information, you are just practicing, because very few will ever call you back. If you just hand people a flyer or a card, don't expect many calls—unless you pass out thousands of them. I'm talking from personal experience, not from theory.

Stop thinking: "How I am going to get this person in my company?" or "How am I going to make this sale?" Just make a friend. I believe a lot of people don't like to talk to new people because they are thinking about how they are going to transition into talking about their business or making a sale.

Here's an example of how to handle this:

(You) Hey, I like that jersey (compliment)!

(Them) Thanks!

(You) Are you a fan?

(Them) Yes, I am.

(You) Yes, me too! Do you go to any of the games?

(Them) No, I wish I could but they cost so much!

(You) Yes, I know what you are saying, but if you did have the means to go, you would go, right?

How to Make Contacts and Win Friends

(Them)   I sure would!

(You)   Well, I can't promise you anything, but I'm working with some local people on a project and ...

OR if they are not a fan:

(Them)   No I'm not. I don't care for them. My wife said this was the only thing clean and I was just running to the store.

(You)   Oh, I see. (Here you don't jump all other the man because he is not a fan of your team; you are out making friends. So, change the subject.) Man I live in XYZ, are you from around here?

(Them)   Yes, I live in WXYZ.

(You)   I'm sorry (as you extend your hand), my name is Carl.

(Them)   I'm Mark.

(You)   Man, we are just around the block from each other and I have never seen you before. Let's keep in touch; we are still neighbors.

Or:

(You)   By the way, have you ever heard of (your business partner's name)?

(Mark)   No, I have not.

(You)   Mark, I'm glad we bumped into each other because he is looking for... Would you or do you know anyone else who might be looking to...? (direct and indirect approach)

You may not have noticed, but in the sentence above, I used both the direct and the indirect approach. I asked if he or anyone he knows might be looking. If you are not comfortable using the direct approach, then practice using the indirect approach. It's less threatening because you are just asking if they know anyone who is looking. You are not asking them if they are looking.

Let's say that you are talking to that person and somewhere in the conversation he mentions a *need* or a *pain* he has in his life. In the back of your mind, make a mental note of what they said so you can bring it back up later if you would like to connect with that person. Here are a few examples of *pain*.

> I'm not too happy with my job.
>
> I like what I do but these hours are killing me.
>
> I would love to take the family on a vacation but I just can't afford it. It's so expensive!
>
> If I could only save for my kid's college...
>
> Man, I wish I could make more money.
>
> If I could afford to get out of these apartments, I would...

If I could only find a better paying job...

I would love to send my kids on a great vacation.

Maybe one of these days I could travel.

Hopefully, I can win the lottery one day.

Maybe my wife can get a second job.

If only things didn't cost so much, I could...

I would love to buy a house.

If a *need* or some type of *pain* is not mentioned while you are talking, you could use probing statements or questions such as:

You must love what you do after 10 years!

Are you pretty close to owning the store by now?
Wow, I bet the owner is about to make you the new boss.

Would you ever want to own the store one day?

I'll bet you will be running the whole franchise soon!

Organize Your Contacts

As soon as you can, make sure that you write some information about your prospect on the back of their card based on your conversation, because you will use some of it on your follow up call.

Example: On the back on the card, write:

Met at football luncheon 12/2/2013.
Son, Matt, is a running back for the Mustangs.
Wife is a lawyer with…
He loves to play golf.

Or, most smart phones have a "notes" tab in the contact section, so you can add a note there, also.

Personally, I have created a note sheet where I copy the information from the back of the card into the comment section, and I also add their info to my cell phone.

Name	Date	Place We Met	Comment	Call Back

Or you can create a table like this one to keep up with your new friends and add what columns make sense to you.

When you call the person back, act as though you've known them for a while: Assume they remember you and just talk like you were old friends.

"Hello _____, this is _____. We met at _____."

(Not, "Can I speak to _____?")

How to Make Contacts and Win Friends

> **Key Points:**
> 1. Don't criticize, condemn or complain.
> 2. Learn to listen.
> 3. Watch your facial expressions.

Take a few minutes to add a few notes of your own based on what you read in this chapter. Perhaps my ideas triggered a few strategies of your own. Take time to jot them down here.

Notes:

_____

_____

_____

_____

_____

_____

_____

_____

Chapter 6

Top Places to Meet People and Make Friends

Get out of your house! You can't meet people in your home. (You can make contacts online, but we're talking old school right now.) Here are a few places that I would suggest for meeting people:

- Faith-based organizations...church, mosque, etc.
- Local classes and seminars
- University and college associations
- Small business development centers (SBDC)
- Your local Chamber of Commerce meetings
- Sporting events
- Service organizations...Rotary and Lions clubs
- Sports bars
- Gyms and workout facilities
- Cultural events

You can serve on committees and organizations that you have interest in; become a board member or chair a committee, volunteer to help, or be a greeter to help direct people. You know what your schedule is like. Be careful not to join so many organizations that you have no time to build your business/company. I would recommend one committee, maybe two, if they only meet once or twice a month. Volunteering is also a good way to meet new people. Help with registration and host an event or move up to the front of the room so you can have a good view of everyone. Helping with new memberships is a great way to meet new members.

Networking Tips

- Get there a little early.
- Always keep the conversation positive.
- When meeting someone new, stand up to greet them.
- Make connections, however, work on business deals at a later date and time.
- Never talk negative about others.
- Learn the art of meet, chat, exchange information then NEXT.
- Don't look like you are over anxious and desperate for business.
- Be excited about being there.
- Afterwards, stay around a little while longer.
- Smile a lot and have fun.

Take time to read up on what's happening with current events, or at least read some general information about that event. In other words, if you're going to a computer event and you know nothing about computers, do a little research to at least have a general knowledge base on how computers work.

A Chamber of Commerce meeting is a good place to meet people and a great resource for new prospects. Sit by the door, that is, by the register table or by the host of the group—the president, or the main speaker, or the secretary—and discover the most popular person there. Most people will talk to other people first, but I always try to talk to the main person there. Introduce yourself and put your hand out to shake his or her hand and, typically, most people will say their name as well. Don't push anyone to tell you their name. If they don't offer, you can always say, "I'm sorry, I didn't get your name."

Watch your attitude, and don't be arrogant! Remember why you are there; be pleasant, be open and be approachable. Finding people with like interests is a good way to meet people, but don't be afraid to veer out and meet others with different interests once you feel comfortable meeting new people. Ask questions so you can learn more knowledge about a new and different subject. It may help you for the next time you talk to someone in that field.

Keep the Flow Moving

Try to avoid that awkward silence, that dead air time. Always be ready to ask a question to help keep the conversation going. Make a comment, ask a question, state something, have several good stories to

How to Make Contacts and Win Friends

tell—but keep the conversation flowing. Also, be ready to have an exit statement ready if the conversation is not flowing well and there's little hope of saving it.

Here are a couple of key phrases to continue the conversation:

"Wow!!! Can you tell me a little more?"

"Will you please elaborate?"

"Do you have any ideas about that?"

"What's your opinion?"

"Oh, did you hear...?"

You will often be in the situation where you need to add something that might relate to the conversation you are having. This is why it so important to read books, listen to CD's, and watch DVD's or movies. Watch good movies with a positive story.

You can also start or get a conversation going by asking questions:

"Where is...?"

"What street are we on...?"

"Do you know where XYZ is...?"

"Excuse me but do you know...?"

"Sorry, I hate to bug you but do you know where ...?"

"Have you seen...?"

"Can you recommend a...?"

"I'm lost, do you know where...?"

Try to stick with one or two subjects when you are talking to new people. Going off on tangents or launching into many different subjects can confuse the person you are talking to. You can always talk about your favorite food, travel destinations, movies, sport teams, or the area you live in.

Here are a few more ways to keep the conversation flowing by asking open-ended questions:

"Donnie, tell me how you got into your line of work."

"What is the part you like best about your industry?"

"What type of trend do you see happening next?"

"Can you tell me a little bit more about your profession?"

"I meet people all the time. Tell me how I would know if someone I meet would be a good contact for you?"

Exercise #2:

Write down two more statements that you can use to start a conversation.

1. _____

2. _____

Have a Few Exit Statements Ready

Always have a few exit statements in the back of your mind. There are two reasons for this:

1. You need to exit the conversation after you find out the information you need.
2. If you don't care for the person you are talking to, you need to have a way to get out of the conversation.

Try to always be in a hurry. Leaders and business owners are always coming from somewhere or heading somewhere, so always be in a hurry. But, don't be in a hurry to the point where you're rushing the conversation, you don't let the other person speak, and you don't learn anything about them. Be patient and polite but always have a few exit phrases ready that pertain to your situation. For instance:

"Mike, I really enjoyed talking to you but ..."

"Mike, I really enjoyed talking to you and I'm about to..."

"Mike, I really enjoyed talking, and I want to continue our conversation, however I ..."

"Mike, I really enjoyed it, but if I don't get out of here..."

"My wife is waiting; let's exchange info because I have to..."

"I have a meeting to get to." or "I'm late for a meeting." (Make sure you do have somewhere to be. Don't just lie.)

"Oh, Mike, there is Charles, and I need to talk to him about ..."

"I don't have a lot of time, can we continue at a later time, because I would really like to learn more."

"Sorry, but I have got to go..."

"I'm running late for..."

"Wow, time has really flown by and I have to ..."

"Oh no, look at the time, I have to go..."

Exercise #3:

Write down two more exit comments you can use to end a conversation:

1. _____

2. _____

You always (and I mean *always*) stay in control of the conversation. If you see the conversation is getting out of hand, back off, exit the conversation, and move on. Remember, you will not get them all. You already have all the tools you need to become an E-A-S-Y Method Specialist. You will just need to practice and get it down. It will become so natural that you will not even realize you are doing it.

Don't Be This Person

Don't cut people off, or say "Yes, I already know that," or "Yeah, I heard all that before." Give them your attention and let them feel as if you just heard it for the first time from them. Remember, you are trying to make a friend, not be a Mr. Know-it-all. Do you know someone who knows it all? You can't tell them anything because they already know everything—so don't be that person. You will not endear people to you by being a know-it-all. You will actually push people away from you.

Don't be so opinionated that you run people off. People are interested in themselves, not in you. So as you are talking to them, wait until you discover some type of *pain* that you can help address later. Just remember, if you do all the talking, you will never find out what *pain* they have.

Don't complain or talk about other people. If you talk bad about other people to them, they may feel you will also talk bad about them to other people.

Have you ever known someone who always knows what is going on? They are always in the middle of negative situations. If you want to find out what's going on, they will somehow know about it. Don't be that person. It will only hurt you in the long run. This is a quick way for people not to trust you. Keep people's personal business to yourself. People will never trust you if you are the person who is passing information around. The funny thing about gossiping or being a know-it-all or being the one who is always in the know is that most of the time they don't even realize it's them, that they're the one who's passing the information around. You don't want to ever be that person; you might think it helps to know everybody's business, but in the long run, and people may not say it, but they will not want to be around you.

Key Points:
1. Get out and network with people.
2. Keep the conversation flowing.
3. Always have a few exit statements ready.

What did you learn from this chapter?

Notes:

Chapter 7

Personality Styles by Color

Different companies use different codes to describe the four major personality styles. Some companies use animal names, some use analytical names, and others use colors.

In time you will learn how to read the other person. Take some time to read other books, listen to CD's or watch DVD's on this topic to learn more.

I have read, listened to, and taken several different personality tests and profiles. The information I am sharing with you is a combination of all the resources I have studied over the years. However, one of the best CD/DVD sets I know about is called "Living in Full Color," by Mr. Marc Accetta.

There are four basic personality styles. You may fall into several areas and overlap styles, but one style will be more dominant than the others. You will be predominantly red, blue, yellow, or green.

If you can learn to master these styles and understand the different behavioral characteristics and adjust your style, you'll be on your way to becoming an E-A-S-Y Method Specialist.

You ask, "What do you mean, Carl?" Well, before I explain how to adjust your style, let me tell you about the four colors:

Red:
Someone with a red style is a person with a driver personality. They are focused on the task at hand, but they are not detail oriented. "Just get it done!" would be something they would say. Most of them are direct, demanding, and tend to take action. Reds are determined, and they have a lot of confidence. They can be very competitive, and they have a bottom line personality, a strong desire to win, and are good decision makers. However, reds can be abrupt, insecure, and selfish—and they may not be team players.

Blue:
A person who exhibits a blue style will be more interactive. They love people and are very friendly. At a party most of the people hang around a blue person because they're probably telling a story or inspiring someone. Blues are outgoing, emotional talkers, and very spontaneous; they love to travel, and they love to have fun. However, they are not good at saving money. And they will show up late—they tend to not to watch the clock much.

Yellow:
If you want to find a loyal friend, find a person who has a yellow style. These people are dependable, and they want to be a part of the team. "What can I do to help out?" would be a question they would ask. They will be the ones who raise their hand when you need a volunteer to help out. Yellows are very stable, and they are good listeners. They are sensitive and very supportive. They are team players, huge on honesty

and integrity, and they are family oriented—they don't like conflict or confrontation; nor do they like phony, materialistic, or greedy people.

Green:

(I'm a red and many [I say many, but not all] reds are married to greens or yellows.) Greens are analytical, detail-oriented people. A green will read *Consumer Reports* back issues for three months before they buy a car. They are cautious and don't want to make the wrong choice. Greens want to know what the numbers say, so they run all the numbers until they add up on a deal; they ask, "Where's the data? Where's the proof?" They do not show their emotions readily. They want to see if something really works, or if it's just a lot of hype. Greens like a plan, a road map to follow, structure—and they don't like surprises; they can be emotionally detached; and they don't make snap decisions.

How to Relate to the Different Colors

To get some practice, study the colors and identify your own dominant color. Then see if you can identify the dominant color of some of your family members and friends.

Exercise #4:

Identify which color you are and write down your three dominant characteristics from the above descriptions:
Your color: _____

1. _____

2. _____

3. _____

OK, I hope you have a good understanding of the four basic personality styles and what your dominate style is.

Now, take some time to learn to adjust to the different behavioral styles. I must admit, this was—and still is—the hardest part of the process.

When talking to a red, it's important that you be direct, get to the bottom line. Try to be as concise as you can. ("Mike, you can make $1,000 next week if you ...") Be straight with a red. They don't mind working if they can see there is a reward. Reds are some of the most successful leaders, period!

If you encounter a blue, put them in touch with other people at a party or at a meeting. "You mean I can make money by talking to other people?" might be something a blue would say. You will not have to get into many details like you would with a green. Just show them that other people are having fun and making money. Show excitement and let them know that they can help so many other people. People love to be around blues.

You will need to take it slow with a yellow. They will need to have some type of security. Yellows want to build relationships, but, because they are loyal and dependable, they want to take time to decide. They want some type of reassurance, so take it slow. You will run a yellow off if you try too hard and move too fast. Let the relationship develop at their pace or you will lose them.

The green type has taught me how to have patience. I'm a red so I want something done yesterday, but that's not the way it works with a green. Gather all the facts, and get all the information you can into their hands so they can review it.

Give them something in a structured form, like a spread sheet on the latest data. It will take some time, but once a green makes up his or her mind, look out! Greens are committed to quality and can be some of your brightest leaders, because once they feel they've made the right decision based on the latest data and facts, they're focused.

To become an E-A-S-Y Method Specialist, you must learn to adjust and mirror the other person's style for a short period of time as you're talking to them.

Example #1:
You're talking with Earl, and you are a red. Earl seems to be a green, so slow down a little and talk about getting all the data that you can for him. Don't talk too fast, and don't move around very much. If he is sitting with his arms crossed, you sit and cross your arms. Just try to relate to his style.

Example #2:
You are a yellow, and you're talking to Michelle. You notice that she is a very strong red. So speak a little faster, and try to develop your relationship quicker by using hard facts and presenting the results, such as: "Michelle, you can make $1,000 next week."

> **Key Points:**
> 1. There are four basic types of personality styles.
> 2. The colors are red, blue, yellow, and green.
> 3. Learn how to mirror people.

Think of some recent contacts you've made and write down your thoughts on what color you think they are and how you should be approaching them.

Notes:

_____

_____

_____

_____

_____

_____

_____

_____

_____

Chapter 8

The Biggest Mistake People Make

The fortune is in the follow-up, and the biggest mistake most people or networkers make is that they don't follow up with their contacts. I talk to people all the time who meet people, get their information and never call them back for one reason or another. Earlier in this book, I wrote about building trust. Trust is the most important thing you want to impart in a conversation. Did the other person feel that he or she could trust you? It's hard for you to really know if they trust you or not, but if you try to help them with their problem (which I call their *pain*) by following up afterward, then you've done your job. Make sure that you follow up with them within 24 to 48 hours, especially if they had a question or needed some information, or if you promised simply to let them know something or to set a date to meet again. Contact them even if it's just to say you're waiting to hear back from someone; show them that you care and you were listening.

When you call back, have the business card with their information or your sheet of notes in front of you. The information you recorded on that card or in your notes is vital. You will need to include something specific in your initial follow-up conversation.

Example: "Hello Roger, this is Carl. It was great to meet you at the ____ yesterday. I enjoyed talking with you. How did Matt do in football practice today?" (Listen...) "Great! Did you ever get that golf game set up for next weekend?" (Listen...) "That sounds good! I hope you have a great time and you'll be at the top of your game. Roger, I talked with my brother, and he knows a man who might be able to help you with... Let's set up a time when we can all talk..."

John C. Maxwell said: "People don't care how much you know until they know how much you care." You will be surprised how many people go straight for the business or the sale. All they see are dollar signs, and in the long run they lose a lot of business. If they would have just slowed down and built a relationship, the dollars signs would have added up.

A good networker will follow up, and he or she will also keep in touch. It may take some time to earn your prospect's trust, but once you do, you will have a friend for life.

Follow up phrases to use at the end of a conversation for getting the contact's number or business card:

"I enjoyed talking to you. Let's exchange contact information and keep in touch."

"Wow! What an informative conversation. I would love to get back with you and continue our conversation. What is the best number I can reach you at?"

"Thanks for sharing! I will call you back in the next few days. Do you have a business card on you?"

"I'm always open to learn more and will follow up with you tomorrow. Let's exchange numbers."

"I will call my brother tomorrow and get back with you ASAP. What is the best time to reach you, and what number do you want me to call you on?"

No Follow-Up = No Relationship = No Business

With today's technology, you have several ways to follow up: email, snail mail, postcards, text, telephone, Twitter, Facebook, and other social media sites. I believe the best way to follow up with a person is to call them because it makes it more personable.

Try to keep in touch with people you meet. After you meet them, stay in touch with them, because things change from time to time and people do business with people they like and trust.

If you call someone several times and they don't call you back within a reasonable amount of time, they are showing you who they really are or they may not want to keep in touch with you. However, if they have something they want to talk to you about, they will call you three times one day. They will track you down!

People will always do what they want to do. People will let you know how they are by their actions. Something I use to say to my sons all the time that's similar to Ralph Waldo's quote is: "Your actions speak so loud, I can't hear a word you are saying." You give first and you will reap in the end if you connect and follow up with a lot of people over the next few months after you meet them.

Many people don't follow up because at the initial conversation there was no real conversation. They didn't learn anything that they could use to start building a relationship. You must use the information you gather and take it to the next step. Use that conversation to build to the next one.

When you call, be respectful of their time; don't just start talking. Ask if they are busy, "Hey Mike, do you have a few minutes? Is this a good time to talk?"

Set a Contacting Goal

Another mistake people make is not setting a contact goal. Some people need to set a specific goal for meeting new people to be able to stay on track. Others have different strategies. I'm not saying that one is better than another. You have to find your own strategy and develop your own comfort level. Let me explain what I'm talking about.

I have a very good friend named Stacye Bowers, and she has mastered the art of contacting new people. Stacye, however, is the type of person who has to challenge herself and set a goal for the number of contacts she makes each week, each month, and so on.

For Example: Stacye will write down *I need to contact x amount of people each day or week.* She will hit that goal about 98 to 99 percent of the time and sometimes exceed her goal, because she is very goal oriented and disciplined. I, on the other hand, find that I don't work that way. I tried that and it didn't work. I found myself in a grocery store at

11:55 p.m. about ready to spear someone down the aisle because I didn't have my goal for that day. So I just use the E-A-S-Y Method with anyone who crosses my path. If it works out, we will connect. If not, NEXT! Stacye's system works for her and mine works for me. You will need to find what works best for you and then just do it.

I will go out on a limb and say that I'm fairly sure your business or company will grow if you use the techniques in this book and then follow up and keep in touch with most of the people you meet. Here is one thing I can assure you 100 percent: If you have zero people on your list and you do not go out and meet new people, your business or company will not grow. However, here you are reading *How to Make Contacts and Win Friends.* So I'm confident that if you apply these techniques, your business will grow.

Add a Minimum of Five People a Week

Think about what making contacts would mean to you and your business or company in terms of simple numbers. If you were to add just one person to your list each day, that would be 365 people a year, 730 people in two years and 1,825 in five years. Yes, that's over 1,800 in five years! But let's cut that number in half, which would be about 912 people in five years, and 365 in two years. Could you use an extra 365 new contacts over the next two years to help you grow your business or company? OK. What if you only met five people a week for a year? Could a potential 260 extra people help you succeed this year?

Circle: Yes   or   No

If yes, then get to work! The longer you put it off, the longer success will evade you. Now let's stop for a few minutes and do a quick exercise. Make a list of the top five places you enjoy going to (church, football games, traveling, live concerts, bowling).

1. _____
2. _____
3. _____
4. _____
5. _____

These are places where you already like to spend your time; plus, they are places where you already know the other people have similar interests.

Exercise #5.

Think of three places and write down the names of five people you know from each place.

Place 1:_____

Name: 1. _____

Name: 2. _____

Name: 3. _____

Name: 4. _____

Name: 5. _____

How to Make Contacts and Win Friends

Place 2:_____

    Name: 1. _____

    Name: 2. _____

    Name: 3. _____

    Name: 4. _____

    Name: 5. _____

Place 3:_____

    Name: 1. _____

    Name: 2. _____

    Name: 3. _____

    Name: 4. _____

    Name: 5. _____

Now create a list of other places you visit and work toward adding them to this list when you can. This is a good way to build a list and continue adding to it. Start today with 15 names and build the list up to 30, even 75 names, continue adding to it each week. Create a spreadsheet in Excel or Word and keep adding to it.

Key Points:
1. The fortune is in the follow up.
2. Set a personal contacting goal.
3. Add people to your list daily or weekly.

Write down a few more follow up phrases and your contacting goal.

Notes:

Chapter 9

You Have to Have This to Succeed

With many years in this industry, I've seen just about everything. There are a few words that come to mind when I think about being successful, like desire and focus. However, there is one thing you have to have to be successful in your business—and that thing is "belief." You need to believe in yourself. Napoleon Hill expressed it best in his book *Think and Grow Rich* (Fortune Publishing Group, 2014). "Whatever the mind can conceive and believe, it can achieve it." Napoleon Hill first published this book during the Great Depression. By the time he died in 1970, it had sold more than 20 million copies, and by 2011 more than 70 million. It has been released in numerous editions, including the latest one I cite above. Hill established a nonprofit foundation as an educational institution to perpetuate his philosophy of leadership, self-motivation, and individual achievement. You can find it at www.naphill.org.

We all have the ability to learn. Some learn faster than others, but we can all learn the skills we need to win—and win big! Always be in a learning mode, and stay hungry for knowledge and apply what you've learned. You can have your dreams and achieve your goals by helping other people with their dreams and goals. But seek out what YOU need to win, not what someone else needs.

Whatever business or company you're in; remember you're in the people business. The more you learn how to deal with people, the more successful you'll become. The more successful you become, the more you'll need to learn how to deal with people.

One of the biggest challenges a lot of people have is – not believing in themselves. You must take the time to learn what it will take for you to believe in <u>you</u>. There are tons of resources and information in the market place today that can help you refine your focus, but you must be able to SEE in your mind's eye all the things you want. You must be able to visualize your goals. So don't limit what you want. Write your goals down, look at them every day, and keep yourself focused.

In his book *From the Hood to Doing Good,* (which I cited in Chapter 3) Johnny Wimbrey mentioned a book titled, See Your Future, Be Your Future, by Terry L. Hornbuckle. "In this book he talks about how important—and how necessary it is—for you to see your future in order for your hopes, aspirations, and goals to become a manifested reality. You must believe without a shadow of a doubt that you deserve to win. And you must practice seeing yourself as the winner in order to be a winner."

There are hundreds of Positive Mental Attitude (PMA) books on the market today, and I personally believe they all have a common theory. You must find a way to believe in yourself through reading, listening to CD's, watching DVD's, and attending personal growth events, such as seminars. Somehow, you have to find a way to block out all the negative images that bombard your mind every day, all the bad news and all the other bad things that happen on a daily basis. Try to limit what negative information enters through your eye and ear gates. Shower your mind with the positive and cleanse it from the negative.

How to Make Contacts and Win Friends

Here is what, I believe, will help you get results if you stay focused. I call it W-B-A-R:

W = Why

B = Belief

A = Action

R = Results

If you have a strong WHY for whatever you want out of your life, you stay focused, and work hard toward achieving it, you can make it happen. Sometimes it might not happen in the time frame you think it should, but if you keep working on it, and keep learning, you will get there.

Somehow, somewhere, at some time as you are working on your WHY, you will also need to believe in yourself. BELIEF gives you the power and the strength to keep going when you feel like quitting. If you have a strong belief in yourself and in what you are doing, you will achieve your goals.

The stronger your belief, the more ACTION you should take. You can have a big WHY and a strong BELIEF in yourself all day long, but without action you just have a why and a belief. If you don't make the calls to your potential clients, customers, or reps, if you take NO action, then you will have NO results! Your results will be zero. People in business are after success, and it takes a lot of action to succeed.

When you know your why, have the belief, and take action, then you will get the RESULTS. Different people get different results at different times. Some are faster than others, but you are not in competition with other people, you are in competition with yourself.

Why--> Belief --> Action -->Results

> **Key Points:**
> 1. Find a way to believe in yourself.
> 2. Read PMA books.
> 3. You must take action.

Write down your WHY and what you want out of life.

Notes:

_____

_____

_____

_____

_____

_____

Congratulations!!! You're well on your way to becoming an E-A-S-Y Method Specialist! You are getting closer!!!

Chapter 10

A Special Message to Network Marketers

NM (Network Marketing) or MLM (Multi-Level Marketing)

I have good news for people who are in network marketing: This industry is only going to get bigger and bigger for many years to come! NM gives you the ability to start your own business. In my personal opinion, a lot of people are looking to be their own boss. Here are ten reasons why I believe NM will only get bigger:

1. You will have a lower start-up cost than a traditional business.
2. You will have the ability to make extra money.
3. Based on work ethic, if you work hard with the right system, you could replace your current income.
4. You will have the opportunity to leverage other people's time and effort.
5. A lot of companies have mentors or leaders who are willing to train you.

6. You can potentially do business in several different states.
7. You can build an international business if the company is oversees.
8. You will have a chance to network and meet other people.
9. You can learn sales and marketing techniques and strategies.
10. You will have the ability to help friends, family, and others create extra income.

I believe a lot of people quit NM once they think they have run out of their warm market (the people they know). If you are in NM, and you feel as if you have talked to everyone you know, you may think you can't WIN. I'm here to tell you that you can still win in NM. There is a BIG gap between talking to people you already know and meeting new people. The reason for this gap is that most people don't have the techniques to learn how to meet new people.

That is where this book comes in. This book will help you bridge that gap and prevent you from quitting. It will give you hope that you can win and win big if you just learn a few new techniques on *How to Make Contacts and Win Friends*. Anyone with a dream, a true dream, can win big. WHY? Because we can all learn new things and make new contacts. The E-A-S-Y Method and the H-C-Q-C Process are the best ways to learn how to meet new people. Don't go out wondering how you are going to entice someone into your business. Go out to make friends.

Get Answers to These Questions Before Choosing a Network Marketing Company

If you are looking at joining a Network Marketing (NM) company, you need to be aware of several questions you will want answered before you sign on the dotted line. Most people get started with people they already know and trust. However, here are a few suggestions to consider before you make your decision. Do yourself due diligence by conducting a little research. This way you will feel assured that you are doing the right thing for <u>you</u>. Network Marketing isn't going anywhere; find a good company and go for it.

Check with the Direct Selling Association (www.dsa.org).

Research the company history.

What type of debt do they have? Are they in the black or the red?

How long have they been in business? (Two to five years or more at least shows some stability.)

Is there a big demand for their product or service?

Has the company plateaued or are their sales still growing?

Have the owners ever worked in the field? Do they understand what it takes to build an organization?

Can you run your business on the Internet or from your cell phone?

What type of training system is in place?

Do they do business worldwide?

How strong is their compensation plan, and what type is it? The four popular plans are: Unilevel, Binary, Breakaway, and Matrix

Find out if the company has a good reputation.

How many levels deep does the compensation plan pay?

What type of leadership is at the TOP, and are they making money?

What type of help and support will you receive? (Bottom line: It's still your business and you have to build it.)

Contact Lists

If you are already in NM, you should have a pipe line of new contacts available to call. I would advise you to have 4 running lists at all times:

1. "Active"
2. "Building Friendship"
3. "Follow-Up"
4. "I Will Prove It"

Keep 10 to 20 new contacts on your "Active" list at all times. These are people you can call on to make your presentation right now.

Keep 10 to 15 people on your "Building a Friendship" list. (For those of you who want to advance to a higher rank more rapidly, keep 50 to 75 names, but the quickest way to get to the top ranks is keeping over 100 names on this list.) This list consists of people you are helping solve a problem, connecting them with other people, or you're just touching base with them until you feel the time is right to move them to your "Active" list.

The "Follow-Up" list is compiled of people you have already talked to, but every three to six months (there are different thoughts in the industry about how long you wait to call them back) you contact them to see if things have changed. It's quite likely that they could be in a different box (explained on page 117) when you call back. The second time you called them they were in box two but six months later when you call them back, they are in box four. Bingoooooo!

There are several ways you can look at the "follow up" list. You decide which one is within your comfort level. Your job is to just expose your opportunity.

- Call them back each week or month.
- Call them back every 3 to 6 months.
- Call them back every year.
- Keep them up to date on your progress.
- Don't call them back at all; just move on.
- Go out and meet new people, create your dreams and they will call you back because you kept going and proved it works.

What you don't want to do is to recycle those same people you have been talking to for years and you stay at the same level year after year.

The "I Will Prove It" list is comprised of all the people who told you your business will not work, those individuals who talked about you behind your back, who told all your friends you are doing something illegal, who want a handout, or maybe just people who don't want anything out of life. The people on this list can help you keep going because you want to prove to them what you are doing works.

I honestly believe that if you use these techniques and you have a good product or service, you can get to the top of your company even if you have zero people on your list right now. Start today and move people through all four lists.

Transition to Business

How are you going to mention your business? Some people go out and try to *get people* into their business right on the spot. I'm not saying that doesn't work, because if you talk to enough people, you will find some that are looking for what you have. However, I say go out and *make friends*.

If you heard about a great price on a pair of shoes or a purse, why wouldn't you tell your friends about it? Well, if you believe in your business and you are excited about it, the first people you would want to tell are your family and friends.

How would you talk to someone you didn't know before you started your own business? You would find something to talk about and start talking, right? If you are in an NM company, there are ways you can make the transition over to your business, once you feel comfortable with the E-A-S-Y Method. Many, many years ago (and still today) the acronym F.O.R.M. was taught in a lot of NM companies.

Family – Occupation – Recreation - Message (or Money)

How to Make Contacts and Win Friends

To help you with your conversation, keep F.O.R.M. in mind as you are talking to new people. If you feel like they are someone you would like to share your business with, mention your message or the money.

Here are two examples of things you might say when you meet somebody new. After I see someone is friendly and I feel that I want to let them know about my business, I will say something like this:

1. "Paul, I enjoyed talking to you. As a matter of fact, I'm working with an organization called (your team or business name). They are a team of business internet owners, and they help mentor people. Do you know anyone who might want to make an extra 3 to 5K this month?" (They respond, "Yes, me!" or "Yes, my brother, Jerry!" Then you continue.) "Well, Paul, let's exchange numbers and I will call you later this week."

2. "Well, Paul, I'm hoping the (his sports team name) will do better next year. Oh, by the way, I'm tied to a group called (your team name) and they are looking for a few people to help mentor. What they do is help people make money utilizing the Internet. If you want to make some money, I can get back to you. What's a good number where I can reach you?"

You can use a combination of these examples or create your own. Just relax and be friendly. You will not get them all, just get the easy ones.

If you have a product or service to offer someone, at the point where you would like to make your transition, give them one or two positive points about your product or service and how it can help them. But don't give them too much information. If you do, they may make a decision without getting all the details.

Here is a list of phrases you can use when talking to people and you need to transition over to your business:

"Wow, that is so funny you said that…"

"Speaking of that, I just…"

"You know, I had something similar happen to me. May I share it with you?"

"If you don't mind, can I tell you…?"

"You might not have heard but …"

"A friend of mine just told me about that same thing. Can I tell…?"

"Do you keep your income options open?"

"I'm working with (company name) and they are expanding."

"I have access to great products that can help you…"

"I have access to a service that will help you save…"

Based on how comfortable you feel, you can use a direct or indirect approach. Just go out and do it until you learn where your level of comfort is. You will never know until you try. You have enough information; you have what it takes; you already have the goods to go for it. Start today. I'm pulling for you!

Create a few of your own transition statements that you feel comfortable with:

_____

_____

_____

You Don't Know What Box They Are In

Keep in mind when you meet or call people that you have no idea where that person might be in life. They are in one of these four boxes:

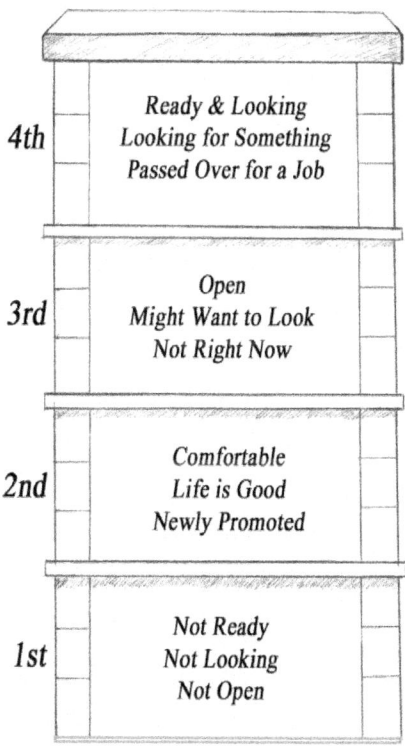

Try to recognize what box they are in at the time you are talking to them. Here are some examples of where that person might be in life and a reflection of what box they're in:

Let's say that you are talking with someone and the subject of working comes up:

- Box 1: I was laid off of work but recently got a new position and I'm totally focused on my new career.
- Box 2: I feel like I have a great job and my boss is real nice to me.
- Box 3: I like where I work but I was passed over for another position. I thought I should have gotten that position so I'm somewhat open to look at something new or different.
- Box 4: This was the third time I was passed over for a position and I even trained the person who got the job, so I am open and ready for a change right now.

Let's say you are talking to someone and the subject of money comes up:

- Box 1: I don't have any money at all and I'm not looking for more.
- Box 2: I don't have a lot of money right now, but I'm working on a few deals already.

How to Make Contacts and Win Friends

Box 3: I don't have much money, but I have some savings. I'm open to at least look.

Box 4: Money is not a problem. However, I'm looking for something to build a better future for my family. I've always wanted a business.

Let's say you are talking to somebody and the subject of travel comes up:

Box 1: We don't travel; we're home bodies.

Box 2: We may take a trip every now and then. We just go to mom's house.

Box 3: We like to travel a few times a year. My wife puts aside money each month.

Box 4: We love to travel and we are looking for some good deals right now!

Listen as they are talking to see which box they are in so you can determine how much time you will spend continuing the conversation. Stay in control; you know the type of people you are looking for. You will get better results if you are connecting with people who are in boxes 3 and 4. However, box 4 is your jack pot and there are plenty of people out there today who are in box 4 right now, so go out and build your business!

Make Your Business System Dependent

My disclaimer to network marketers is this: If your leadership is teaching you something different from what I'm about to say, and it's working for you, continue to follow your leaders.

You will want to make your business system dependent and not people dependent. In NM or Multi-Level Marketing (MLM) you are taught to edify (to build up, lift up, or talk good about) your leaders and others in your business. The art of edification when done right is one of the biggest secrets to building and keeping a BIG business in NM. However, be careful how you edify others. You can always find something good to say about someone, just do it in degrees; don't say things that are not true. If you tell people things that are not true, it will come back to haunt you one day. So, a word of wisdom: Learn how to edify, but don't lie.

> Example:
> Someone you are working with buys a new car. You go around telling your team they bought a new car and they paid cash for it. You say they added a special package that cost an extra few thousand dollars. That sounds good, and it will get some folks excited. However, someone found out that they didn't pay cash for it, that they are making payments on it each month. Also, the special package was only a few hundred dollars. Now your credibility is in question. Just be honest and don't say or repeat something that is not true.

The bottom line is always be a person of integrity. If you are saying things that are not true, I assure you sooner or later you will be found out, and people will not trust you. So if it's not true, don't say it. Hard work can get you to the TOP, but the right type of character will keep you there.

Whatever your particular business, there is most likely some system in place. (If not, find someone to help you create your own system.) Help guide your team through that system, and teach them to do the same to their new people. You want to duplicate the system over and over to win, and win big.

Most companies already have system tools in place: CD's, DVD's, magazines, websites, videos, company training programs, seminars and major events.

In other words, you help guide your team to use the company's system or your leadership's system to help grow and sustain your business. If you concentrate all your efforts toward certain people or yourself, then people only grow when you or that person is around. However, if you concentrate your efforts on the system, people will learn to also guide new people to that system. Then, when you or your leaders are on the beach enjoying family time, your business will still be growing because the system will be working for you.

I'm not saying don't edify, because no man is an island to himself. What I am saying is to edify people, but don't build your total business around yourself or that person. Learn the skill to edify and guide your team to a system that can help you grow your business when you are not there. That is freedom—and you can have it if you build your system right.

Hard Facts About Network Marketing

As I mentioned earlier in this chapter, I believe network marketing will only get bigger and bigger. On the blog mlmattorney.com, the article, *Network Marketing: A Growing Industry, Hard Facts and the Future* (Reprinted with permission of author Jeffrey Babener, copyright 2012), addressed the facts about NM.

Hard Facts and Demographics about a Growing Industry from 2006. (These facts are constantly changing but are reflective of the immensity of the direct selling industry.)

- Every week, more than 55,000 people in the United States alone sign up as network marketers—150,000 per week worldwide.

- In excess of 13 million people in the United States alone are distributors for network marketing companies; one in ten households have a direct seller.

- Throughout the world, there are approximately 50 million network marketing distributors.

- In the United States, sales in the network marketing industry are in the $30 billion range. Worldwide sales approach $90 billion.

- The world leader in network marketing is the U.S. with Japan in close pursuit in the $20 to $30 billion range. Countries with at least $1 billion in sales include the U.K., Brazil, Italy, Germany, France, Canada, and Taiwan. Business is booming in the new frontiers as well: Eastern Europe, Russia, and the People's Republic of China. In fact, Amway in 2004 is headed for $2 billion in China, a country only on the brink of formally allowing the reintroduction of network marketing.

- Seventy-five percent of all network marketing distributors are women. Men account for 25 percent. (These numbers likely reflect the demographics of long-dominant companies like Avon and Mary Kay. Recent growth in the industry has been among newer companies that have a more even balance between male and female distributors.

- Approximately 80 percent of networkers are part-time and 20 percent are full-time people who work 30 hours a week or more in their business. For the vast majority of networkers, it is a "second job," with the hope of earning $300 to $500 per month in auxiliary income.

- About three percent of all networkers make more than $35,000 a year; two percent make more than $50,000; 0.5 percent make more than $100,000 annually; and about 0.1 percent make more than $150,000.

- About 13 percent of direct marketers are African-American; almost five percent are Latinos; one percent are Asian; and about 0.5 percent are Native Americans.

- Approximately 66 percent of distributors are between ages 25 and 44. Another 14 percent fall into the 45 to 54 age bracket. Seniors over the age of 65 account for about five percent of direct sellers.

- About eight percent of direct sellers have physical disabilities.
- Over two-thirds of all network marketers have high school degrees or some college education, and 25 percent have a college degree or beyond.

The Future Is Up

So, where is the NM business going? The answer is "UP." During the next decade, the Direct Selling Association projects that network marketers will recruit more than 200 million new distributors into the business worldwide.

Do you believe NM will continue to grow? Why?

Notes:

_____

_____

_____

_____

_____

_____

_____

Chapter 11

Online and Social Media Marketing

I will be the first to say that lots of people have made money doing online marketing only. I can also say that there are a lot of people who have not made one dime online. I have personally spent a lot of money doing only online marketing and, while I'm not saying it doesn't work, I'm saying I never got it to work to the level I wanted it to. If you are one of those people too, don't be ashamed; it's just a stepping stone to your success.

Use the Internet to make it easier to connect with people—then call the person after you make the connection. Treat them like a human being and keep in mind that the Internet is only a tool to create a real friendship. You will need to talk to the people you are connecting with.

Online marketing gurus teach you to send at least two or three emails a day to your list. They say it is easy to find content to send to your list. Yes, there is a lot of information available; but just sending unrelated content to people is not an effective way to spend your time.

By the time you look up content, put an email together, and set it up, you could have met two people using the E-A-S-Y Method. You can succeed using online techniques, but it takes time, patience, and constant communication with people on your list. Plus, you have to try to sell them something from time to time.

Information and technology change with time; and you need to at least have some knowledge of what's changing, because there is one constant, and that is change. Be willing to learn new technology and at least have some knowledge about how it works.

When contacting someone online, check their profile, their pictures, their friends, LinkedIn, Facebook, etc. See who they are connected to. If you don't care for what's on their wall, leave them alone.

Connecting Online

When you use the Internet to connect with new people, it is called traffic or leads. There are lots of ways to create traffic or leads on the Internet. Some leads are created for free and others cost you money.

We live in a world of social media. People think they can just post a message online and become rich and make all this money from Facebook, Instagram, Twitter, and LinkedIn. By just posting on my wall or in my groups, I will become successful—this is the mindset some gurus convey to people. Let me just say, that is not always the case. Use these online sites as a connecting or reconnecting resource, then use your email and get contact information to call them.

Remember to rebuild a little of the friendship or relationship first before you jump right into talking about your business or your company. If something comes up while you're rebuilding that friendship, or some type of *pain* in their lives comes up, let them know you might have a solution for them—but focus on rebuilding the relationship first. People do business with people they like and trust.

Internet Resources You Can Use to Create Leads

Craigslist—place frees ads

Create a blog—like a website but you can interact with and get comments from other people

Banner Advertising—one of the first types of lead generators; they are located on a lot of websites in a graphic form (picture)

Google adwords—ppc advertising (pay-per-click)

Bing ads—using the Google search engine

Facebook advertising—ads to the right hand-side of your Facebook page

Join into a forum—position info on a forum

YouTube—video marketing

Groups.google.com—all of your discussions in one place

Twitter—social networking and microblogging service that utilizes instant messaging, SMS (short message service)

Instagram—online photo-sharing, video-sharing and social networking service

Tumblr—microblogging platform and social networking website

Tagged—allows members to browse the profiles of other members, play games, and share tags and virtual gifts

LinkedIn—social networking website for people in professional occupations

There are many, many more on the internet, and you can find one that suits your interest.

If you want to post ads for free, here are a few sites you can post on.

Article Directories

Buzzle.com

Articlesfactory.com

Ezineartical.com

ArticleAlley.com

GoArticles.com

ArticlesBase.com

Here are more ways you can generate leads.

More Lead Generators

Link swapping. If you have a website or blog, swap your

link with someone else in order to help support one another.

SEO (search engine optimization)—using key words

Press release—use a wire system

Writing articles and submission to directories

Social book marketing sites—digg.com, reddit.com, squidoo.com and technorati.com

Viral marketing—write an ebook or free report

Video marketing—Vimeo—YouTube

LinkedIn—business people

Podcast—set up a podcast

Pinterest—interests, and hobbies

Write down several other internet resources you can use to create new leads.

Notes:

_____

_____

_____

_____

_____

Chapter 12

Bonus Chapter:

The Secret to Attracting Leads Who Will Request You on Facebook

I'm using Facebook as an example in this chapter, but you can use this method on many other social media sites with the same results.

Treat Facebook as if you were at a networking event. For instance, when you first walk into the room, you wouldn't walk up to the stage and blast: "Hello! My name is Mike, and I can show you all how to get more leads and make money." That's exactly what you would be doing when you blast a post on a Facebook page/wall, on a group page, or on a friend's wall. Don't do it!

At a networking event, you would walk around meeting people and exchanging information and business cards. Your message inbox is like a business card; you are looking to connect with a request or send a request to your new friend.

There are many great books about learning how to relate and win friends, but the one I recommend you read is Dale Carnegie's *How to Win Friends and Influence People*. Carnegie presents three fundamental techniques for handling people:

1. Don't criticize.
2. Don't condemn.
3. Don't complain.

When you are posting on Facebook, remember those three C's. You are trying to attract friends—the right type of friends. You want to bridge the gap and build a friendship. Connect with them and see if you can help solve their challenge.

If you remember this principle, you will have enough leads requesting you all the time. You will be adding value to a person's life—and you will have as many friends as you can ever handle.

Carl Randolph

Five Steps to Build a BIG Lead List Online

Step #1:

Before you start joining groups, make sure you have high quality content to offer. Make sure you take the time to create content that can add value and be relatable to your target audience. If you are a golf pro, for example, and you don't like tennis, then don't join tennis groups; join golf groups.

Step #2:

Search for and join active groups you can relate to. Take a few minutes to look around each group and see what it's about and who is a part of it. Some groups are open and some are closed. The open ones will accept you right away, but the closed ones have an administrator of the group who will need to accept you into the group.

Once you are in, you may want to introduce yourself with something short, such as: "Hello. My name is Mike, and I'm excited about joining your group. I'm looking to learn and add some value, also."

Then you will want to add good content—information, videos, free reports, articles, and the like.

How to Make Contacts and Win Friends

Step #3:

Be patient. Once you've been accepted in the group, remember, you are new to the group, so be a little patient. Some people will want to check you out first before they contact you. If your content is of high quality and will add value to their life, they will request you.

Step #4:

Once someone requests you or hits the like button, you can connect with them. Look at your notification tab at the top, left corner. It will show you all the activity. (Add a picture to your post and you will be able to see your post faster in the notification by your picture.) First, look over their profile and their friends. Check them out; look for something in common that you can relate to and that will spark a conversation.

Send a message to their inbox or chat with them if they are online. Don't post on their wall. You want to send a more personal message in their inbox. Provide a little information about yourself also, to keep the conversation going. Always, always end with a question at the end of your message. This will keep the conversation going. For example: "How are you doing today?" "Did you watch the game?" or "Are you looking forward to a big year ahead?"

Step #5:

Look for what I call *pain*, or an opening. Once you feel that this is someone you would like to connect with, you request them or confirm their request. Ask questions that will give you a way to solve their situation. You are a problem solver; so help solve people's problems and you will have people requesting you all day long.

Follow these steps and you will have no problem adding new leads to your Facebook contacts or to any other social media site you are a part of.

> **Key Points:**
> 1. Treat your online contacts like offline contacts.
> 2. Join groups you can relate to.
> 3. Send a message to their inbox or use the chat.

Write down what groups you would like to join. Can you think of any content that would add value to those groups?

Notes:

_____

_____

_____

_____

_____

_____

_____

_____

Putting It All Together

As I said in my introduction, my goal is to help you. If I have accomplished this, I feel it was well worth the time and effort for me to share my techniques with you. My sole intention for writing this book has been to help people who are struggling with meeting new people. I hope and pray I have accomplished that. I hope you will use the techniques I provide in *How to Make Contacts and Win Friends* to do exactly that: make contacts and win friends for life! So now, let's sum this up!

Just Say "Hi!"

We should be about helping people. So, if you're standing there thinking, "I could possibly help this person with the *pain* that he or she might be experiencing in their lives right now," and you don't say anything—you will never know if you could have helped them or not. I'm 100 percent certain that that person in front of you will not be a new contact or a new friend if you don't say anything. They won't look at you and think: "That man has a business or company and I need to talk to him." That just doesn't happen! So focus on building relationships and friendships, then on making money.

Use Both Old School and New School Marketing

I understand what all the online marketers are saying. Over the years, I have made thousands of cold contacts using the three foot rule. There's a wave of "new school" thinking, but I believe you have to approach making contacts the right way to win. Treat your online contacts, such as those on Facebook and LinkedIn and any other social media site, just like you treat your offline contacts. Build a friendship first.

In my opinion, if you only focus on making online contacts, you may miss finding the next biggest leader in your organization or company, someone who may have been standing right in front of you at the store yesterday. If you only think about online marketing, you wouldn't have said a word to that person. Remember, every person you meet could potentially lead you to hundreds, maybe thousands of additional contacts.

Be smart and utilize both old school and new school marketing. Why leave money on the table or a chance to help somebody else. You can win! You can do it! Set a goal for your business or company and focus on that goal. Start each day with your goal in mind, and go for it! As the Nike commercial says: "Just Do It!"

It's All About People

Every business needs clients, customers, members, or reps. Whatever you call it, it still comes down to PEOPLE. Whatever business or company you have, you need people to generate money and to be successful. People are everywhere, every day, but how do you get them to buy into your product or your business or your service? The answer is by befriending them first and seeing if they are a match for you.

The Personal Touch

I have personally used the E-A-S-Y Method to meet thousands of people. Whether you use an online or offline approach, make sure you pick up the phone and talk to people. The personal touch may seem old-fashioned (I know we live in a world of social media), but I still truly believe people like the personal touch. People are still people, and they want to feel special—some need to feel special. At the end of the day, however, the Internet is still not personal. People like to be talked to. You can master the E-A-S-Y Method and memorize all the techniques, but if you don't apply what you learn, this will just be another book.

Build Friendships

The better you are at creating a friend, the faster you can do business. Developing relationships with others can be slow and steady or fast, but you can't control that. Create little tricks that will help you remember people and find a way to keep in touch.

The one thing I can tell you is that if you are in business or have any kind of company, you will need a way to add people to make that business successful. So, the faster you get started, the faster you will be able to meet new people. Treat people like people with feelings and emotions. Build friendships (the right way). Make people feel like they are people and not just a contact on a computer.

If you learn the techniques for how to meet new people, you will never run out of names, and you will always be able to create a new list. Your business will never die—it will only grow.

Choose Your Topics of Conversation Wisely

When you are talking to someone for the first time, be careful if the subject turns to politics or religion. Views can vary from person to person. Always remember, you are trying to make a friend or a connection, so getting into a debate about really personal issues, such as religious views, can't help.

Stay clear of politics, religion or anything that can turn the conversation into a battle or controversy. Let people have their opinion because it's still their opinion. If you totally disagree but you still want to connect with them, listen and nod your head. (I'm not saying don't stand on your beliefs, I'm just saying this might not be the time or place.) Ask yourself: "Do I want to be right, or do I want to make a friend? Do I want to be successful with people who only think or believe like me?"

Follow Up and Follow Through

If you have gathered a lot of business cards but you have no relationship or no connection with those individuals who gave them to you, you just have a lot of business cards. I have met thousands of people over the years, and I have stacks of cards. Some of them I have done a good job of keeping in touch with and others I have not, but I keep moving forward. If you are not building relationships, you are missing out—however, you can start today.

Be a person of your word. If you say something, do what you say. If you tell someone that you are going to call them, make sure you call them when you said you would. Following up and following through with someone is key. You will lose credibility with people fast if you say one thing and do another.

Just Be You

As you continue to grow, you will become a leader within your business or company. You will start to attract people because people are looking for leaders. People are hungry to be led. The more you start to understand people and how they think, the faster and more professional you will become when it comes to meeting new people. Remember, people are just people; some are good, some are bad, some are friendly—and some are not. You don't know which ones are friendly until you say something. Stop caring what other people think about you; just go out and be friendly—and meet some new people.

Dream Big

Focus on mastering the E-A-S-Y Method, and the more people you meet, the faster you will grow—period! You know what you want but you take what you can get. You will have obstacles in life, but if you make your dreams bigger than your obstacles, and you stay focused, you can get there. Whether you have no problem meeting new people or you are shy, I truly believe this book can help you succeed.

If We Can, You Can

I have tried it all. I have written articles and submitted them to hundreds of article directories. I created a personal blog and added lots and lots of content. I have spent an appreciable amount of money on books and software packages. I have listened to CD's, watched DVD's, and spent many hours on webinars and conference calls.

I hope the techniques I share in *How to Make Contacts and Win Friends*, the techniques I use to meet people, will turn your contacts into friends or business partners. If I can, you can! My prayer is that you will take the techniques you feel most comfortable with and apply them into your everyday life. Remember Lashette, Brandon, and Lynette? If they can, you can!

I hope I can meet you one day, and you will say that this book helped you get out of your comfort zone and be a better conversationalist with people. Maybe it helped you to understand that meeting someone new is not as hard as you thought it would be or that it helped you to build a bigger business.

If you know someone that could also take advantage of the techniques described here, have them order a copy today at http://HowToMakeContactsAndWinFriends.com.

In Conclusion

Let me leave you with this short story to keep in mind as you are using what you have learned in this book.

> A young man noticed his wife was just lying around one day. He asked her if she was feeling OK and she replied, "No, I have a bad headache, and I need some ABC aspirin." Not even thinking twice, he jumped into his car and drove to the nearest grocery store. He picked up a bottle of ABC aspirin and proceeded toward the checkout counters. As he approached the checkout counters, he realized he didn't have his wallet with him, but he did have a $5 bill in his pocket. The price on the ABC aspirin was $4.75, so with tax, the price would be about $5.15. There were about 15 checkout counters but only eight were open. He was worried about his wife and didn't want to go all the way back home so he walked up and down the aisle looking at each cashier and stopped at the last one. He explained his dilemma to the cashier and he said he would be glad to come back and pay her the difference, but without hesitating, she said, "Don't worry. I will take care of the difference." He thanked her after she checked him out and as he walked away, she said, "Excuse me, sir. Can I ask you a quick question?" He replied, "Sure, you can!" She said, "Of all the cashiers here, why did you come to me?" He said, "It was simple. It was your eyes. I could see the kindness in your eyes and I just knew in my spirit you would help me."

As you continue to meet people and use the techniques you learn in this book, you will be able to see the kindness in the right people's eyes. You will know who to talk to and who not to talk to. However, there are a lot of people out there who are skeptical. One of my friends and mentors, Wayne Nugent, is a master at meeting people and has been for many, many years. He has no problem walking into a room and meeting people. Sometimes he will just walk up to someone, pull out a $100 bill and say, "I will give you this $100 bill for a $20 bill." He says that most of the time, they will ask what's wrong with the $100 bill? He says, "Nothing, but I'm not going to offer it to you again." Wayne's message is simple. Some people are just not going to accept your offer and they are not the ones you are looking for.

Folks, I would have to agree 100 percent with one of my other mentors, Matt Morris. He always says it's just a numbers game and you just have to go through the numbers. He is absolutely right!

Be willing to stay focused on your dreams and goals, and just go through the numbers. Your numbers will be different from someone else's, because we all have our own numbers we have to go through. The good news is that we can ALL succeed. There is no way of getting around it: Meeting new people and building relationships will add to your bottom line.

Congratulations! You are now an E-A-S-Y Method Specialist!

Disclaimer and Terms of Use

The author and publisher of *How to Make Contacts and Win Friends* offers no guarantees or promises regarding income. Any techniques or strategies used by individuals are at the discretion of each person. This book is for educational and informational purposes only. The author and the publisher do not accept any responsibilities for any liabilities resulting from the use of the information and techniques contained herein. While the publisher and the author have used their best efforts in preparing this book, they make no representations or warranties with respect to the accuracy or completeness of contents of this book and specifically disclaim any implied warranties of merchantability or fitness for a particular purpose. No warranty will be created or extended by sales representatives or written sales materials. The advice and strategies contained herein may not be suitable for your situation. The publisher is not engaged in rendering professional services, and you should consult with professionals where appropriate. Neither the publisher nor the author shall be liable for any loss of profits or to her commercial damages, including but not limited to special incidental, consequential, or other damages.

Bibliography:

Wikipedia.com

From the Hood to Doing Good
Johnny D. Wimbrey (2003, Brown Books Publishing Group)

How to Win Friends and Influence People
Dale Carnegie (1981, Pocket Books)

Skill with People
Les Giblin (1995)

The Unemployed Millionaire
Matt Morris (2009, John Wiley & Sons, Inc.)

CPSIA information can be obtained
at www.ICGtesting.com
Printed in the USA
LVOW04s1745240416
485095LV00029B/993/P